THE
EARLY CAREER
FRAMEWORK
HANDBOOK

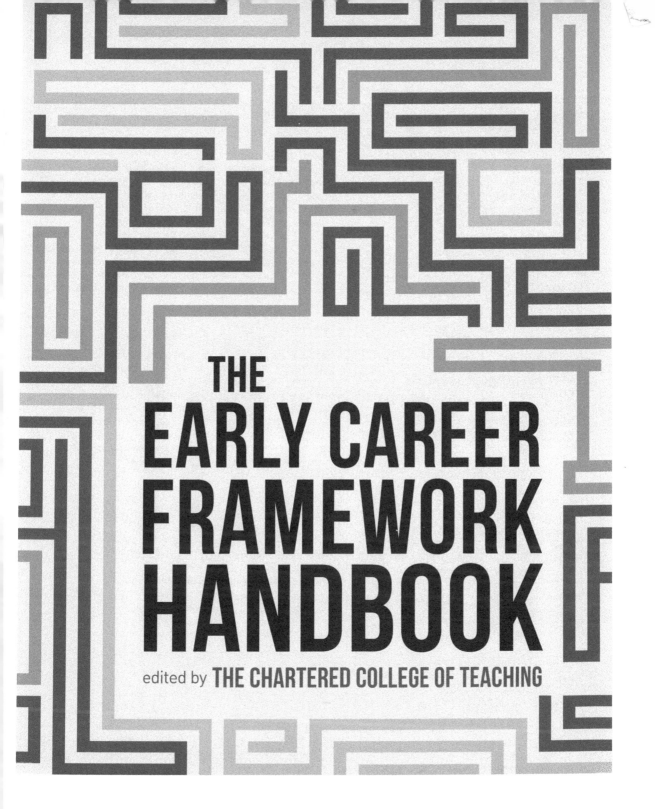

THE EARLY CAREER FRAMEWORK HANDBOOK

edited by **THE CHARTERED COLLEGE OF TEACHING**

CORWIN

A SAGE company
2455 Teller Road
Thousand Oaks, California 91320
(0800)233-9936
www.corwin.com

SAGE Publications Ltd
1 Oliver's Yard
55 City Road
London EC1Y 1SP

SAGE Publications India Pvt Ltd
B 1/I 1 Mohan Cooperative Industrial Area
Mathura Road
New Delhi 110 044

SAGE Publications Asia-Pacific Pte Ltd
3 Church Street
#10-04 Samsung Hub
Singapore 049483

Editor: Amy Thornton
Senior project editor: Chris Marke
Project management: Swales and Willis Ltd,
Exeter, Devon
Marketing Manager: Dilhara Attygalle
Cover design: Wendy Scott
Typeset by: C&M Digitals (P) Ltd, Chennai, India
Printed in the UK

First published in 2020

Library of Congress Control Number: 2020903717

British Library Cataloguing in Publication data

A catalogue record for this book is available from the British Library

ISBN 978-1-5297-2457-8
ISBN 978-1-5297-2456-1 (pbk)

At SAGE we take sustainability seriously. Most of our products are printed in the UK using responsibly sourced papers and boards. When we print overseas we ensure sustainable papers are used as measured by the PREPS grading system. We undertake an annual audit to monitor our sustainability.

CONTENTS

ABOUT THE CHARTERED COLLEGE OF TEACHING

The Chartered College of Teaching is the professional body for teachers. We are working to celebrate, support and connect teachers to take pride in their profession and provide the best possible education for children and young people. We are dedicated to bridging the gap between practice and research and equipping teachers from the second they enter the classroom with the knowledge and confidence to make the best decisions for their pupils.

Through Chartered College membership, teachers have access to a wealth of research, resources and insight to enable excellent teaching. From termly issues of our award-winning journal, *Impact*, and our Chartered Teacher programme, to exclusive events and countrywide networks connecting teachers to collaborate, members have access to the tools to constantly develop their skills and teaching expertise. By bringing the profession together and giving teachers a platform for their voices to be heard and their expertise to be respected, we can raise the status of teaching together.

ABOUT THE CONTRIBUTING AUTHORS

Christian Bokhove is Associate Professor at Southampton Education School, University of Southampton. He specialises in mathematics education, technology use and research methods. He can frequently be found on social media contributing to the educational debate.

Adam Boxer is the Head of Science at the Totteridge Academy in North London. Adam is particularly interested in applying findings from cognitive science and other branches of psychology to the classroom. Adam is the managing editor of CogSciSci and has presented nationally and internationally for ResearchEd. Adam is an active member of the Chartered College of Teaching and has been published in *Impact* on a number of occasions, as well as contributing resources to a number of Chartered College training programmes.

Ryan Campbell is High School Vice Principal at Jakarta Intercultural School. He has lived mainly in Indonesia since 2001. He is interested in human behaviour in organisations and international education.

Faye Craster has worked in teacher education for 11 years. At Teach First, she is responsible for leading all work relating to developing teachers. This includes leadership of Teach First's core training programme – recruiting, placing and developing 1,700 teachers each year to work in schools where they are needed most.

Megan Dixon is Director of English at Aspire Educational Trust and Co-Director of Aspirer Research School. Megan is fascinated by how we can transfer research evidence into effective classroom practice and is often reading research and working with researchers to develop practical strategies to transfer their work into teaching and learning. She is always involved in at least one research trial (currently studying for a doctorate) and is a regular TES contributor.

Sarah Earle leads the Teacher Assessment in Primary Science (TAPS) project at Bath Spa University. After 13 years teaching in primary schools, she became a senior lecturer for Primary PGCE in 2012. She is also a Primary Science Quality Mark senior regional hub leader and a founding fellow of the Chartered College of Teaching.

Velda Elliott is Associate Professor of English and Literacy Education at the University of Oxford. She was an English teacher in state schools in Yorkshire before undertaking doctoral research at the Oxford University Centre for Educational Assessment, gaining her doctorate in 2011. Velda researches in the fields of English in education and educational assessment.

Mark Enser has been teaching geography for 16 years in a range of schools from Gloucestershire to Sussex and as a head of department for the last six years. He is also the author of *Making Every Geography Lesson Count* and *Teach Like Nobody's Watching*, as well as a regular TES columnist.

Jonathan Firth is a psychology teacher, author and researcher. He works on the University of Strathclyde's teacher education programmes. His research interests include professional research engagement and the practical applications of memory and metacognition research to education. He writes school psychology textbooks and support books for teachers.

Amy Forrester is a teacher of English and Director of Pastoral Care with responsibility for behaviour at Key Stage 4. She has led on significant school improvements on behaviour as well as delivering training on behaviour management. She regularly speaks at educational conferences and is a TES behaviour columnist.

Niki Kaiser is a chemistry teacher and research lead at Notre Dame High School in Norwich. Prior to this, she worked as a postdoctoral researcher in marine biogeochemistry. She is particularly interested in finding ways of applying educational research evidence within the classroom, and blogs regularly about teaching and learning at **bit.ly/KayeChem**.

Simon Knight is Joint Head Teacher at Frank Wise School in Banbury, a school for children aged between 2 and 19 with severe or profound and multiple learning disabilities. He is also a national SEND leader for Whole School SEND, a consortium of organisations committed to enhancing the quality of education for learners with special educational needs and/or disabilities.

Reuben Moore is Executive Director at Teach First. He is responsible for a range of programmes for teachers, leaders and schools. He taught and led in schools for ten years and served on the DfE's expert advisory group that developed the Early Career Framework and the Initial Teacher Training Framework. He is Chair of Governors at a local primary school.

Nienke Nieveen is an associate professor and a director of the teacher education programmes at the University of Twente, the Netherlands. Her orientations are in teacher professional learning in relation to curriculum (re)design in schools. Nienke chairs the EERA curriculum network and is an associate editor of *The Curriculum Journal*.

Mark Priestley is Professor of Education at the University of Stirling and Director of the Stirling Network for Curriculum Studies. His research interests lie in the school curriculum – theory, policy and practice. He is a lead editor of *The Curriculum Journal* and a co-convener of the EERA network 3, curriculum.

Alex Quigley was an English teacher for over 15 years in a large secondary school in York. After taking on a variety of school leadership roles, he became an author and columnist for teachers, specialising in literacy and evidence-based practice. He now works for an educational charity.

Pritesh Raichura is Head of Science at Michaela Community School in London, and blogs regularly about teaching and learning, science-specific pedagogy and literacy ideas at **https://bunsenblue.wordpress.com**.

Nasima Riazat is a business studies teacher, author and researcher. She works as a middle leader at Pendle Vale College, where her role comprises of teaching and leading PHSE, careers, RSE and citizenship, as well as leading the school's BTEC vocational programmes. Nasima's research interests include educational leadership and exploring cognitive science strategies to support learning.

Nick Rose is a fellow in learning design at Ambition Institute and co-author of *What Every Teacher Needs to Know about Psychology*, published by John Catt.

Cat Scutt is Director of Education and Research at the Chartered College of Teaching. A former English teacher, Cat's roles have since focused on supporting teacher development, with a particular focus on development through collaboration and through engagement with research and evidence. Cat leads on the Chartered College of Teaching's work around teacher development and certification, including the Chartered Teacher programme, and their research activities and publications, including their award-winning peer-reviewed journal, *Impact*.

Clare Sealy is Head of Curriculum and Standards for the States of Guernsey. She is interested in the application of cognitive science in the classroom, what it tells us about memory and how this could influence how we plan for long-term learning through coherent curriculum design. She blogs about how schools might go about putting educational research into practice at **www.primarytimery.com**.

Marc Smith has taught in secondary schools across Yorkshire since 2004. He is the author of *The Emotional Learner* and co-author (with Jonathan Firth) of *Psychology in the Classroom*. Marc is a regular contributor to TES, where he writes on topics related to psychology and learning.

Andy Tharby is an English teacher at a large secondary school in West Sussex who also trains teachers and leaders in ways to implement evidence-informed strategies in schools. He is the co-author of *Making Every Lesson Count* and the author of *Making Every English Lesson Count* and *How to Explain Absolutely Anything to Absolutely Anyone*.

Rob Webster is an associate professor based in the Centre for Inclusive Education, UCL Institute of Education. He researches and writes on the topics of inclusion, special educational needs and teaching assistants. Rob also works across the sector to help schools improve the deployment and impact of teaching assistants.

Karen Wespieser is Director of Operations at Driver Youth Trust. Karen has worked in education for 20 years. Most recently, she was Head of Impact at NFER and Director of the Centre for Education Economics. She is passionate about increasing and communicating the use of evidence in education. Karen is also a school governor and a trustee of Parentkind.

Bukky Yusuf is a senior leader, science teacher and consultant. She has undertaken a number of leadership roles within mainstream and special schools and is also an ambassador for Leadership Matters. Bukky is also a network leader for WomenEd. As a qualified coach, Bukky is actively involved with a number of grassroots educational set-ups, including BAMEed and the wellbeing initiative #Teacher5ADay.

1

MANAGING BEHAVIOUR EFFECTIVELY

AMY FORRESTER

DIRECTOR OF PASTORAL CARE (KS4), COCKERMOUTH SCHOOL, CUMBRIA, UK

INTRODUCTION

Without excellent behaviour, there cannot be excellent learning. It is the bedrock of everything in a school. It can also be the most challenging part, and an area where you may find you need some support. Remember that behaviour is never straightforward – we're dealing with children! Everyone has struggled with it at some point, and it's important that you tackle this head-on right from the off. That's why the Early Career Framework (ECF) has a whole section devoted to it – it is complex and challenging, but ultimately it is the most important area that we have to get right in order to ensure that no time is lost when it comes to learning. Young people only get one chance at an education, and every minute matters. Drawing on the work of Lemov (2015) and Marzano and Marzano (2003), this chapter will help you to explore the ways in which the ECF sections will apply to your day-to-day teaching and help you to inform your steps with behaviour management.

> ### CHAPTER OBJECTIVES
>
> By reading this chapter, you will understand:
>
> - where, how and why to implement routines in your day-to-day teaching;
>
> - the importance of verbal and non-verbal communication in managing behaviour and known strategies for managing this in the classroom;
>
> - how to deliver instructions in a way that contributes to a positive classroom atmosphere;
>
> - how to work positively and proactively with colleagues on ensuring excellent behaviour;
>
> - the importance of consistency, both within your own classroom and as part of the whole-school ethos and culture, and how to get the right support with this.

ROUTINES

Routines are a vital part of successful behaviour management. When routine becomes habit, it makes managing behaviour far easier for you as a classroom teacher. Once students know what is expected of them in your lessons, the opportunity for poor behaviour diminishes. It is also vital that you remember routines need to be explicitly taught, reinforced and modelled until the desired standard is achieved. Even then, you will need to continue to do this. Children sometimes get out of habits or decide to challenge expectations – they're children, after all!

The first place to start with routines is to work out all of the possible opportunities for routines to become embedded in your lessons. As a minimum, you should be looking at:

- entry to lessons;
- beginning of lessons;
- transitions between tasks;
- end of lessons.

ENTRY TO LESSONS

You need to consider what your expectations are for students' entry to your lesson. It is the first opportunity to reinforce the idea that you are in control of their behaviour. You might wish to consider the following: *Do you want students to line up silently first? What should students do when they enter your classroom? What should they be doing in order to be ready to learn in your classroom? How will you know that students are doing this?*

BEGINNING OF LESSONS

A positive start is imperative. This can be most easily achieved by ensuring that students know what they need to be doing at this point. Having a learning task for them to get stuck into immediately is one way of making this achievable. You might wish to consider the following: *How can you use the first task to help students retrieve or practise their knowledge? What can you do to make this as simple as possible?*

TRANSITIONS BETWEEN TASKS

Depending on your subject and phase, this will vary. In order to make this effective for you, spend some time considering the following: *What transitions do you commonly have within your lessons? How much time should these take? How could you improve the speed/efficiency of these to ensure that no time is wasted in the pursuit of learning? Are there any health and safety considerations?*

END OF LESSONS

The end of lessons provides you with an opportunity to assert control within the classroom. Consider how best to demonstrate this. Commonly, this might be students standing silently before they are dismissed, but there makes it infinitely harder for a school to achieve good behaviour. Children need to understand what behaviour is expected in the school as a whole. Teaching is a team sport – you and all of your colleagues to be following the policy in the same way, otherwise the policy is meaningless. This means that people will be fighting their own battles in isolation, and ultimately the only loser in this is learning. Therefore, it's vital that you take time to understand your school's behaviour policy so that you can implement it consistently. Some things that you might want to do to help with this are as follows.

SPEAKING WITH THE SENIOR LEADERSHIP TEAM (SLT)

The first place to start in ensuring you are implementing the policy appropriately lies in discussions with senior leaders. Generally speaking, schools will have a senior leader with overall responsibility for behaviour. Start with them. Take along some pointers for discussion, such as an example of where you think you have followed the policy well (ask them if you are correct) and an example of where you are not sure that you are in line with the policy (ask to discuss this with them and find out what their thoughts are). You might also want to ask them about which staff they believe are implementing the policy well.

OBSERVING OTHERS

Once you have found out who is using the school policy well, seek them out and ask to observe them. Sometimes it can be hard to see a policy in use, especially where behaviour is good. Instead, look for things such as the following: *What is the normal expectation of behaviour? How are students behaving throughout the lesson? How does this compare to behaviour and expectations in your lessons?*

BEING OBSERVED

A really useful strategy for refining or improving your own consistency can come from inviting colleagues to observe your lessons, with consistency and behaviour management as the specific focus for the observation. This does not have to be a formal observation; it can be an informal drop-in to see how you're doing. Generally speaking, the best person to do this would be the person with overall responsibility for behaviour.

KEY QUESTIONS

- How do I define excellent behaviour?
- How is excellent behaviour defined in my school?
- What areas of my practice are strong? How do I know this? Would others say the same?
- What are the ways in which managing behaviour differs among teachers?
- How can my approach be enhanced by the practice of others?

They will have the clearest vision of how the policy should look in use on a day-to-day basis, and they will be best placed to give you specific, informed feedback on where you are with consistency, as well as giving you some useful pointers for improvement.

CONCLUSION

In summary, behaviour is one of the important things you will need to master. It also takes time, patience, support, personal reflection and deliberate practice. It is important to remember that no one suddenly becomes a qualified teacher and is perfect at it. Every teacher will have, at some point in their career, found it challenging, and you will be no different.

Remember these key points:

- Improving routines is a quick win for any classroom teacher. Identify all of the opportunities for routines in your lesson, and devise and deliver them to your classes.

- Getting support can make a big difference quickly. Start by talking to someone you trust about your behaviour management and make use of their support and advice.

- Reflecting on explicit delivery can make a big difference. Before your lesson, think about how you will phrase your instructions. Identify how they could be made more precise and where they could include expectations about behaviour.

KEY CONCEPTS AND FURTHER READING

CLASSROOM MANAGEMENT

Lemov, D. (2015) *Teach Like a Champion 2.0: 62 Techniques That Put Students on the Path to College*. San Francisco, CA: Jossey-Bass.

- This is a hugely influential text which explores the classroom management techniques that led to excellent learning outcomes in the US.

Marzano, R.J. and Marzano, J.S. (2003) The key to classroom management. *Educational Leadership*, 61(1): 6–13.

- This article explores the evidence surrounding classroom management techniques that teachers can use to improve behaviour.

STRATEGIES TO IMPROVE BEHAVIOUR

Bennett, T. (2010) *The Behaviour Guru: Behaviour Management Solutions for Teachers*. London: Continuum.

- This excellent book by the government's 'behaviour tsar' is packed full of strategies.

KEY QUESTIONS

- Think of a lesson you taught recently where the students were highly engaged. How did you know they were highly engaged? What physical signs were there?

- Philosophically, is motivation an end in its own right? If students finish a course of study with good results but low motivation, has the teacher or school failed in some way?

All of these things are *observable behaviours*, things that you can see a person is actually doing. Whether they actually do love you, though, is less certain. You cannot know for sure and can only infer from their observable behaviours what is going on in their head. Those observable behaviours become *proxies* for love, ways of us establishing a mental state by inference.

Like love or any other emotion, learning is an invisible mental process that can be thought of as an increase in students' long-term memories (Kirschner et al., 2006). We can never know for sure if learning has taken place as we cannot see inside our students' heads. What we can do is elicit *observable behaviours* in our students and try to *infer* whether learning has occurred. Teachers might do this in several ways, perhaps predominantly by simply asking students a question. If a student responds accurately to my asking, 'What is the definition of a salt?' then I might infer that the student has learnt the definition of a salt. Their response allows me to infer that they have learnt.

Over time, many have lost sight of the nature of this inference, and instead allowed the observable behaviour to become a proxy for learning. Instead of thinking about the learning that has taken place, we look for the observable behaviour and are satisfied when we see it, forgetting that it only allows us to make inferences.

In a landmark paper, Professor Robert Coe (2013) decried the use of poor proxies for learning in the classroom. He argued that students completing lots of work gives no indication of whether or not learning has occurred. The quality of work in the short term and revisiting that work in the long term were both necessary conditions to establish if learning had taken place. Observing a large volume of work being completed is no more proof of learning than buying flowers is proof of being in love. For our purposes, the most important poor proxy that Coe discusses is engagement. Student attentiveness or focus might be necessary conditions for learning, but these alone do not cause learning to occur. There is so much more to the complex and long-term project of learning than student engagement in one lesson or activity.

Coe is complemented well here by the work of Graham Nuthall (2007), whose observational studies of hundreds of classrooms led him to conclude, 'Our research shows that students can be busiest and most involved with material they already know. In most of the classrooms we have studied, each student already knows about 40–50% of what the teacher is teaching' (p24). Engagement not only fails to give you positive data about student learning, but in fact can give you negative information; it can trick you into thinking that students are learning something new when in fact their engagement is a function of their *not* learning anything new at all. As such, the target I set myself as an NQT was a particularly bad one as activities to boost student engagement could have tricked me into thinking that far more learning was taking place than there was.

KEY QUESTIONS

- In what ways do you gather data to establish whether learning has occurred?

- How confident are you in your inferences about student learning?

- In a lesson where students were highly engaged, how can you be sure that they were making forward progress?

WHAT IS THE DISTINCTION BETWEEN INTRINSIC AND EXTRINSIC MOTIVATIONS?

It is important to define two phrases used extensively throughout the research literature on motivation: intrinsic and extrinsic factors. 'Intrinsic' generally relates to things that come from within the student, such as their personal beliefs and attitudes (e.g. they think science is fundamentally interesting or a worthy pursuit in and of itself). 'Extrinsic' generally relates to things that come from outside the student in order to motivate them (e.g. a parent committing to give a student a financial reward for particular grades).

There is, by now, a vast literature on the use of rewards to affect extrinsic motivation (Willingham, 2007), and coverage of that literature is beyond the scope of this chapter. However, summarised below are a number of important findings that can impact on what you do in the classroom. It is also worth noting that recommendations regarding the use of extrinsic rewards are only ever general rules of thumb. They do not apply to all students all the time, and part of your becoming a more experienced practitioner is identifying the conditions under which each is effective.

LIMIT 'IF-THEN' REWARDS

This type of reward is given by the teacher as a certainty following a particular activity or achievement (e.g. 'If you finish this essay before the end of the lesson, then you will receive x'). The most significant problem with rewards is that the activity becomes tied to the achievement. If the student does the activity and gets rewarded for it today, they are less likely to do it again tomorrow in the absence of a reward (Kazdin, 1982).

A further problem is the potential for the least compliant students to get the most rewards. If a teacher encourages a student who is not currently working to work for a reward, the student then receives a reward for something the other students did without having to be incentivised. This might then have a toxic effect on the other students, leading to their becoming disillusioned or non-compliant in order to gain the same rewards.

BE VERY CLEAR ABOUT MEETING EXPECTATIONS

Do not reward students for meeting baseline expectations. If a student says something such as, 'Can I have a reward point as I did well today?' then the response should be, 'You have met my expectations, just like all the other students. You don't get a reward for doing what you were supposed to.' This way, students will not become habituated to rewards.

REWARD EFFORT, NOT ACHIEVEMENT

Imagine a student is promised a reward for scoring 80 per cent in a test. They work hard in preparation but don't quite hit the 80 per cent. It's likely that in the future they are going to work less hard, suspecting that they are just going to fail. At the same time, a student who did not work hard but scored 80 per cent will resent not receiving a reward. It becomes more of a judgement call, but saying to the first student, 'I'm so proud of how hard you worked – have this reward' and, 'You didn't work hard enough, and I know you can do better – you won't get a reward until that point' to the second might lead to more positive outcomes.

WHEN USING REWARDS, GIVE STUDENTS THE MEANS TO SUCCEED

In a study assessing the impact of financial incentives on student outcomes, researchers found that in many cases, the financial incentives did increase student effort, but there was no resultant increase in student outcomes (EEF, 2014). This could be because students were directing their efforts to ineffective study habits, by now a well-researched phenomenon (Dunlosky, 2013). If you are going to incentivise students to complete an activity, ensure that the activity is an effective one.

KEY QUESTIONS

- Think of a recent time when you rewarded a student. Did that student deserve a reward more than the students who did not receive a reward?

HOW CAN SELF-DETERMINATION THEORY EXPLAIN WHY SOME TEACHER ACTIVITIES LOWER STUDENT MOTIVATION?

Self-determination theory (SDT) is a theoretical model that aims to holistically encompass all the factors that lead to an individual's long-term motivations. One of the key pillars supporting it is called *competence*, and it relates to how competent – or 'good at' – an activity a person is. SDT argues that we tend to enjoy things at which we are competent and not enjoy things at which we are incompetent.

A very clear classroom example of this is the use of setting in the classroom. Research shows that students in 'lower' sets can feel disenfranchised and unmotivated (EEF, 2018), perhaps unsurprisingly, given the message they have been given about their competence.

HOW CAN SELF-DETERMINATION THEORY EXPLAIN WHY SOME TEACHER ACTIVITIES INCREASE STUDENT MOTIVATION?

The flip side of the above is that theoretically, if a student's competence can be increased, their motivation might increase in tandem. This theory has been put to the test by researchers who have found that competence does predict motivation (Garon-Carier et al., 2016; Nuutila et al., 2018). Students who were motivated in a subject at one point in time did not necessarily enjoy positive outcomes in that subject later on. However, students who enjoyed positive outcomes in a subject at one point in time did later develop positive feelings towards it, even if they cared little for it at the beginning.

Another interesting source of evidence for this proposition is Project Follow Through (PFT), an enormous study costing millions of dollars, which proved that the teaching strategy of direct instruction (DI) showed enormous academic gains compared with many other forms of teaching, including ones focused on group work, inquiry and softer skills – traditionally thought of as more engaging. It is worth noting that DI not only outperformed these other forms on academic measures, but also on ones that measured students' feelings and motivation to study (Barker, 2019). Put simply, the programme that helped students learn the most (i.e. become the most competent) was also the most motivational.

In the same vein, having students in a 'bottom set' isn't by necessity a bad thing. If a practitioner carefully sculpts the class's trajectory over time, uses clear and explicit instruction, and slowly allows students to feel some success in a subject, then an increased motivation may follow (Black, 2019).

CONCLUSION

Engagement and motivation are complex games of short- and long-term variables. Engaging activities might bring short-term gain, but over the long term are less likely to lead to the difficult business of learning.

Activities that increase the chances of successful learning might seem to be not particularly exciting, but over the long term can lead to a deep and enduring love of a subject, rooted in the feeling of competence that springs from conquering demanding content. You must be wary to balance these competing factors in the classroom, and find a way to bring students to a point where they work hard for you not because they seek reward or find the work easy or fun, but because they are intrinsically motivated to do so.

KEY CONCEPTS AND FURTHER READING

PROXIES FOR LEARNING

Willingham, D. (2010) *Why Don't Students Like School?* San Francisco, CA: Jossey-Bass.

- This book explains the cognitive and biological processes underpinning thinking and includes practical strategies to support student learning.

INTRINSIC AND EXTRINSIC MOTIVATION

Didau, D. and Rose, N. (2016) *What Every Teacher Needs to Know about Psychology*. Woodbridge: John Catt Educational.

- Didau and Rose outline some of the most useful psychological principles that teachers should be aware of – Part 2 is on motivation and behaviour.

THE RELATIONSHIP BETWEEN COMPETENCE AND MOTIVATION

Barker, S. (2019) How direct instruction can improve affective factors. In A. Boxer and T. Bennett (eds), *Explicit and Direct Instruction*. Woodbridge: John Catt Educational, pp109–16.

- This chapter explains the relationship between competence and motivation, and what this means for classroom practice.

REFERENCES

Barker, S. (2019) How direct instruction can improve affective factors. In A. Boxer and T. Bennett (eds), *Explicit and Direct Instruction*. Woodbridge: John Catt Educational, pp109–16.

Black, J. (2019) *Delivering a Knowledge-Rich Curriculum to a 'Bottom Set' Year 9*. Available at: https://cogscisci.wordpress.com/2019/09/05/delivering-a-knowledge-rich-curriculum-to-a-bottom-set-year-9/

Coe, R. (2013) *Improving Education: A Triumph of Hope over Experience*. Available at: www.cem.org/attachments/publications/ImprovingEducation2013.pdf

Dunlosky, J. (2013) Strengthening the student toolbox. *American Educator*, 37(3): 12–21.

Education Endowment Foundation (EEF) (2014) *Increasing Pupil Motivation*. Available at: https://education endowmentfoundation.org.uk/public/files/Projects/Evaluation_Reports/Pupil_Incentives.pdf

Education Endowment Foundation (EEF) (2018) *Setting or Streaming*. Available at: https://educationendowment foundation.org.uk/evidence-summaries/teaching-learning-toolkit/setting-or-streaming/

Garon-Carrier, G., Boivin, M., Guay, F., Kovas, Y., Dionne, G., Lemelin, J.P., et al. (2016) Intrinsic motivation and achievement in mathematics in elementary school: a longitudinal investigation of their association. *Child Development*, 87(1): 165–75.

Kazdin, A. (1982) The token economy: a decade later. *Journal of Applied Behavior Analysis*, 15(3): 431–45.

Kirschner, P.A., Sweller, J. and Clark, R.E. (2006) Why minimal guidance during instruction does not work: an analysis of the failure of constructivist, discovery, problem-based, experiential, and inquiry-based teaching. *Educational Psychologist*, 41(2): 75–86.

Nuthall, G. (2007) *The Hidden Lives of Learners*. Wellington: NZCER Press.

Nuutila, K., Tuominen, H., Tapola, A., Vainikainen, M.-P. and Niemivirta, M. (2018) Consistency, longitudinal stability, and predictions of elementary school students' task interest, success expectancy, and performance in mathematics. *Learning and Instruction*, 56: 73–83.

Willingham, D. (2007) Should learning be its own reward? *American Educator*, 31(4): 29–35.

3

SETTING AND MAINTAINING HIGH EXPECTATIONS

MARC SMITH

AUTHOR, INDEPENDENT RESEARCHER, CHARTERED PSYCHOLOGIST AND ASSOCIATE FELLOW OF THE BRITISH PSYCHOLOGICAL SOCIETY, UK

INTRODUCTION

High expectations form the foundations on which effective teaching is built. Teachers have the ability to affect pupil outcomes in many ways, and what they do on a daily basis will impact not only academic achievement, but also related concepts such as wellbeing, motivation and behaviour. As a newly qualified teacher (NQT), you have the chance to create and nurture a classroom environment that supports learners of all levels through high standards as well as an emphasis on hard work, shared values and support. Your pupils should feel challenged, but they should also understand that setbacks occur, and that they possess the capacity to overcome them, move on and flourish. High expectations help to safeguard pupils from anxiety and fear of failure.

CHAPTER OBJECTIVES

In this chapter, you will learn how to:

- create a positive classroom culture based on high expectations and shared values where every pupil, regardless of background, is challenged and supported;

- ensure that your own behaviour reflects the attitudes, values and behaviour you expect to see in all pupils;

- nurture a culture of mutual trust that supports and respects effective relationships where making mistakes and learning from them are accepted and overcome through effort and persistence.

CREATING A POSITIVE CLASSROOM ENVIRONMENT

The right classroom climate helps to create an environment of trust and mutual respect, and one where effort, determination and high expectations are valued and actively pursued. Organisational structures and learning practices can help to create this by, for example, ensuring that teaching is organised in a way that encourages persistence and determination, even in the event of setbacks. Monitoring in-class demands, fostering positive interpersonal relationships between both pupils and teachers and pupils and peers, and shared goals and values help to encourage a positive classroom culture. Aspects of learning such as school-related ambition and expected effort can be encouraged through shared goals and values, both within the classroom and the wider whole-school environment.

All pupils need to be aware of what is expected of them if learning is to be effective, and these expectations need to be communicated using effective language. Intentional language that conveys clear learning outcomes (such as challenge, aspirations and related goals) helps to maintain an environment that encourages persistence and motivates pupils. Consistently returning to these expectations ensures that beliefs around self-efficacy, appropriate behaviour and persistence become embedded within the day-to-day routines that further encourage and promote positive academic outcomes. In addition, building predictable routines helps to curtail unwanted behaviours.

WELLBEING

Positive and supportive classroom environments help to nurture general wellbeing. Pupils who feel supported and valued display higher levels of academic-specific resilience or academic buoyancy (Martin, 2013). Lower levels of wellbeing can result from teacher and pupil expectations that are both too high and unmanageable and too low, so expectations should be high yet manageable and supported through the use of challenging goals.

Pupils often communicate their levels of wellbeing through their behaviour and emotional responses, which can be severe in circumstances related to fear of failure and extreme worry. However, seemingly negative emotions such as anxiety can serve a useful purpose by increasing motivation. Low levels of anxiety are therefore necessary, yet when levels of anxiety pass this optimum level, the stress response can begin to negatively impact on limited cognitive resources, memory can become impaired, and attention wanes (Smith and Firth, 2018, p14).

MOTIVATION

Motivated pupils learn faster and more efficiently and have a greater desire to engage and remain attentive. Motivation is a combination of biological, emotional, cognitive and social factors that can all be enhanced by creating a positive classroom culture. Specific emotional responses (e.g. anxiety and boredom) can dampen motivation and lead to fear of failure and worry over appearing unintelligent, so those pupils who struggle should be supported through effective guidance and feedback.

Motivation can be viewed as either intrinsic or extrinsic. Intrinsic motivation is fuelled by a desire to engage in a task for its own sake, perhaps through interest and curiosity. Extrinsic motivation relies on the expectation of (often tangible) rewards. When intrinsic motivation is low, rewards can help, but if intrinsic motivation is high, rewards can backfire and lead to a drop in motivation (Lepper et al., 1973).

Motivated pupils are able to maintain focus and attention for longer, either because they find the area of study intrinsically interesting or they view the material necessary for the pursuits of individual learning goals. For example, a pupil might be hoping to study a subject at a higher level in order to achieve some further academic or occupational goal. While they might not find the current topic of study interesting or engaging, the pupil can be encouraged to view the topic as necessary in the long term, and this realisation fuels motivation further.

According to a model of motivation known as self-determination theory (SDT), teachers who support pupils' basic psychological needs of autonomy, competence and relatedness nurture autonomous self-regulation, academic performance and wellbeing (Niemiec and Ryan, 2009). This means that at times, you will need to step back and allow pupils the opportunity to regulate their own learning, face individual setbacks and challenges, work through problems, and recover from struggles and disappointment.

BEHAVIOUR

Managing behaviour in the classroom requires a positive classroom culture and the consistent use of rewards and sanctions. Poor behaviour can be indicative of low wellbeing, reduced levels of motivation, and feelings of not being in control of outcomes; however, this isn't always the case. As a teacher, you have the ability to ensure appropriate behaviour that encourages learning is maintained through routines and consistent use of behaviour management policies.

KEY IDEAS

- Increasing levels of motivation doesn't mean that you have to make all your lessons fun. Consider ways that you can make topics relevant or how you might tweak your pupils' curiosity.

- Effective behaviour management is a key component of a positive classroom culture. Continually ask yourself if your actions are consistent, such as if you are applying the same rewards and sanctions to all pupils, regardless of who they are.

SELF-REFLECTION: BEING A ROLE MODEL

Your own behaviour will reflect what you expect to see in your pupils. Children and young people acquire an understanding of appropriate behaviour by observing the social interactions of others; this will include their peers and aspects of the wider environment such as the media. However, they will also shape their behaviour by observing adults with whom they come into contact, particularly teachers.

When you behave in a positive or socially acceptable manner, your pupils will pick up on these behaviours and assimilate them into their own behavioural blueprints. To model positive learning strategies and acceptable behaviour, you should display this behaviour in the classroom and reward others who adhere to these standards through praise and encouragement.

KEY QUESTIONS

- Are you a good role model? Reflect on how your daily behaviour would look from another person's perspective and then consider if this is the kind of behaviour you would wish to see in others.

- Think about the behaviour you witness in your classroom. Is this behaviour learnt from peers, significant adult others or sources such as the media?

A CULTURE OF MUTUAL TRUST

Classrooms should represent a culture of mutual support, respect and trust. High-quality teacher–pupil relationships are linked to higher academic standards as well as increased wellbeing. This is particularly the case with young children, but longitudinal studies have also discovered that the connection between positive relationships and learning outcomes continues throughout schooling.

While nurturing positive relationships has been found to raise levels of both academic achievement and general wellbeing, relationships that are negative in nature and with a high instance of conflict can lower wellbeing and deplete the cognitive resources necessary for learning (Spilt et al., 2012). Pupils thrive in classrooms with a positive atmosphere and those with effective management strategies. Furthermore, pupil–teacher relationships are more effective when parents are in regular contact with the school (O'Connor, 2010), so a brief phone call or email home reporting on pupils' progress can reinforce good relationships.

A classroom where every pupil is supported and relationships are positive also impacts pupils' fear of failure. Mistakes and setbacks are inevitable consequences of learning, yet often they are seen as negative. Fear of failure can negatively impact academic and wellbeing outcomes as pupils attempt to safeguard their self-esteem through maladaptive strategies, including procrastination and self-handicapping (sabotaging or placing insurmountable obstacles in their path). Pupils may feign illness, deliberately ensure they are unprepared, or refer to internal traits and dispositions as a way to excuse any possible future failure. Pupils may also set themselves unachievable goals, so in the event of failure, they can claim that it was because their standards were too high.

Setbacks can result in feelings of disappointment and guilt, so creating a positive environment where failure is accepted can move pupils away from fear-oriented behaviour. Pupils who accept setbacks as inevitable display higher levels of academic buoyancy, not because they think they won't fail, but because they are confident in their ability to bounce back (Putwain and Symes, 2012). Studies have also found that highlighting the struggles of key historical figures such as Albert Einstein can help to highlight the importance of failure for eventual success (Lin-Siegler et al., 2016).

> ## KEY QUESTIONS
>
> - We all experience setbacks and failures, but it's how we react to them that matters most. What are the things that help you recover after a setback, and can you use this experience to help create a positive classroom environment?
>
> - Some pupils are more failure-avoidant than others, and this can impact different aspects of their behaviour. How might fear of failure manifest in some pupils?

HIGH STANDARDS FOR ALL

Higher levels of education are linked to several positive outcomes, particularly higher incomes, better health and wellbeing, a more favourable position in the labour market, and a lower risk of poverty (OECD, 2015). Teachers should therefore hold the same high expectations for all pupils and understand that lowering expectations for disadvantaged groups may negatively impact their future life trajectories. You should never be tempted to set less challenging goals and tasks for pupils you may perceive to be less equipped to deal with the challenge.

THE SELF-FULFILLING PROPHECY

Having high expectations for all pupils will increase their capacity to engage and display greater levels of academic buoyancy. Conversely, if you expect pupils to underachieve, this can result in your own unconscious behaviour reinforcing feelings of failure. If you assume that a pupil will achieve, there is a tendency to treat that pupil differently than one who is expected to underachieve, which in turn can influence academic outcomes, a phenomenon known as the self-fulfilling prophecy (Rosenthal and Jacobson, 1968).

Expectations are guided by previous academic outcomes and other non-academic attributes unique to the pupil. If, for example, you are of the opinion that girls are more studious, conscientious and well behaved than boys, this can potentially lead to subtle yet far-reaching changes in the way you respond to them. Holding high expectations for some pupils based on arbitrary beliefs can lead to the halo effect. We can't help but make these assumptions about people in general, but being aware of these biases can go a long way to ensuring that they don't impact negatively on the learning outcomes of pupils.

Another way to avoid acting upon these biases is to rely on performance data rather than subjective opinions, especially as studies have found that pupils are often aware of teacher expectations (Rubie-Davies et al., 2014). By holding equally high expectations for all pupils based on previous achievement and combining this with challenging yet manageable goals, you can avoid many of the pitfalls associated with both the self-fulfilling prophecy and the halo effect.

THE IMPORTANCE OF GOALS

Setting goals that challenge and stretch pupils is a vital part of maintaining high standards. Goals increase motivation by providing a very specific target to work towards; however, setting the goal might provide an intention to compel it but may lack the actual implementation (the plan that guides goal pursuit). You therefore need to ensure that pupils both know what their goals are and offer them guidance on how to get there. Goals increase motivation and encourage self-regulated learning. Pupils who are skilled at self-regulated learning feel more in control of their progress and are able to cope more effectively with setbacks, because self-regulated learners explicitly work towards their goals and adapt their behaviours and attitudes when things don't go the way in which they expect.

The emphasis is therefore on both autonomy and control, where pupils are in a position to monitor, direct and regulate actions towards their goals, including those related to information acquisition, the expansion of expertise and self-improvement. Feelings of control place success in the hands of pupils, emphasising the importance of personal effort on academic achievement, increasing their ability to take on more challenging tasks (Lazowski and Hulleman, 2016). In turn, this helps to raise self-efficacy – the belief in their ability to successfully complete a given task.

KEY QUESTIONS

- We all hold biases about a range of things, but being aware of why we hold such unconscious beliefs can help us keep them in check. Think about your own beliefs about why some pupils achieve while others don't. Does this change your attitude towards them?

- Do you set your own goals, and is the way you approach them effective? Goals might be achievement, personal or career-directed, or they might be in the form of New Year's resolutions. Why might such goals remain unrecognised?

CONCLUSION

This chapter has discussed the need for high expectations and the important role they play in academic achievement. As a teacher, you create a classroom culture where all pupils, regardless of their background, are given an equal chance to thrive and succeed, supported by an environment that encourages determination, conscientiousness and the pursuit of challenging yet achievable goals. In addition, by supporting pupil wellbeing and nurturing positive teacher–pupil and peer relationships, you can shape a classroom environment where setbacks and mistakes are viewed as an important part of the learning process. Key concepts to remember include the following:

- A positive classroom climate supports pupil wellbeing, motivation and appropriate behaviour that encourages all pupils to achieve, as well as raising levels of academic buoyancy.

- High-quality teaching, along with a culture of clear expectations and goals, supports all pupils, particularly those from disadvantaged backgrounds.

- Effective teacher–pupil relationships arise from a culture of mutual trust where pupils accept the inevitability to make mistakes and learn from them.

KEY CONCEPTS AND FURTHER READING

MOTIVATION

Niemiec, C.P., Ryan, R.M., Pelletier, L.G. and Ryan, R.M. (2009) *Autonomy, Competence, and Relatedness in the Classroom: Applying Self-Determination Theory to Educational Practice.* Available at: http://selfdeterminationtheory. org/SDT/documents/2009_NiemiecRyan_TRE.pdf

- This article discusses elements of self-determination theory and examines the link between students' basic psychological needs and their academic engagement and learning outcomes.

ROLE MODELS

Johnson, S.K., Buckingham, M.H., Morris, S.L., Suzuki, S., Weiner, M.B., Hershberg, R.M., et al. (2016) *Adolescents' Character Role Models: Exploring Who Young People Look up to as Examples of How to Be a Good Person.* Available at: https://dl.tufts.edu/concern/pdfs/1831cw53b

- This research paper uses findings from a study involving 220 adolescents to examine the impact of a variety of role models on the character development of young people.

WELLBEING

Education Endowment Foundation (EEF) (2016) *Building Social and Emotional Learning into the Classroom.* Available at: https://educationendowmentfoundation.org.uk/news/building-social-and-emotional-learning-into-the-classroom/

- This post reflects on a report from the Public Policy Institute of Wales around school-wide approaches towards building emotional resilience in children and young people.

CLASSROOM CLIMATE

Rathmann, K., Herke, M.G., Hurrelmann, K. and Richter, M. (2018) *Perceived Class Climate and School-Aged Children's Life Satisfaction: The Role of the Learning Environment in Classrooms.* Available at: https://journals.plos. org/plosone/article/file?id=10.1371/journal.pone.0189335&type=printable

- This study offers an insight into school-aged children's perception of the classroom climate, taking into account a variety of factors such as teacher care and involvement, monitoring, autonomy and interaction.

REFERENCES

Lazowski, R.A. and Hulleman, C.S. (2016) Motivation interventions in education: a meta-analytic review. *Review of Educational Research*, 86(2): 602–40.

Lepper, M.R., Greene, D. and Nisbett, R.E. (1973) Undermining children's intrinsic interest with extrinsic reward: a test of the 'overjustification' hypothesis. *Journal of Personality and Social Psychology*, 28(1): 129–37.

Lin-Siegler, X., Ahn, J.N., Chen, J., Fang, F.-F.A. and Luna-Lucero, M. (2016) Even Einstein struggled: effects of learning about great scientists' struggles on high school students' motivation to learn science. *Journal of Educational Psychology*, 108(3): 314–28.

Martin, A. (2013) Academic buoyancy and academic resilience: exploring 'everyday' and 'classic' resilience in the face of academic adversity. *School Psychology International*, 34(5): 488–500.

Niemiec, C.P. and Ryan, R.M. (2009) Autonomy, competence, and relatedness in the classroom: applying self-determination theory to educational practice. *Theory and Research in Education*, 7(2): 133–44.

O'Connor, E. (2010) Teacher–child relationships as dynamic systems. *Journal of School Psychology*, 48(3): 187–218.

Organisation for Economic Co-operation and Development (OECD) (2015) *Do Teacher–Student Relations Affect Students' Well-Being at School?* Available at: www.oecd-ilibrary.org/docserver/download/5js391zxjjf1-en.pdf?expires=1498563087&id=id&accname=guest&checksum=C6582D9178CD2FC390213CD60876BB8E

Putwain, D.W. and Symes, W. (2012) Achievement goals as mediators of the relationship between competence beliefs and test anxiety. *British Journal of Educational Psychology*, 82(2): 207–24.

Rosenthal, R. and Jacobson, L. (1968) Pygmalion in the classroom. *The Urban Review*, 3(1): 16–20.

Rubie-Davies, C.M., Weinstein, R.S., Huang, F.L., Gregory, A., Cowan, P.A. and Cowan, C.P. (2014) Successive teacher expectation effects across the early school years. *Journal of Applied Developmental Psychology*, 35(3): 181–91.

Smith, M. and Firth, J. (2018) *Psychology in the Classroom: A Teacher's Guide to What Works*. London: Routledge.

Spilt, J.L., Koomen, H.M.Y., Thijs, J.T. and van der Leij, A. (2012) Supporting teachers' relationships with disruptive children: the potential of relationship-focused reflection. *Attachment & Human Development*, 14(3): 305–18.

PART 2

SUPPORTING LEARNING AND DEVELOPMENT

4

UNDERSTANDING MEMORY

NICK ROSE

FELLOW IN LEARNING DESIGN, AMBITION INSTITUTE, UK

INTRODUCTION

Section 2 of the Early Career Framework (ECF) relates to understanding 'how pupils learn', but what does the term 'learning' mean? We can easily contrast learning with innate behaviours such as reflexes; a change in light levels will cause your pupils to change size, but you didn't learn to do this – it is a reflex response. Learning, according to the American Psychological Association, can be defined as involving a lasting acquisition of new behaviours or knowledge, based on experiences (APA, 2018). An important part of the process of learning involves attending to relevant aspects of our environment, mentally processing this information and integrating it with what we already know, and these processes involve memory.

In order to help you get to grips with 'how pupils learn', this chapter will explore how learning and memory are related, including discussion of 'working memory' and 'long-term memory', the role of prior knowledge, and the importance of practice and review in helping pupils to consolidate their learning.

CHAPTER OBJECTIVES

Psychologists' understanding of these components of memory and learning have arisen from decades of research, and this chapter will, by necessity, provide a very basic introduction to the topic. However, it is hoped that by the end of this chapter, you will have:

- developed your understanding of the role of attention in learning;

- considered the limitations of working memory, including cognitive load, and some of the implications this may have for teaching;

- understood the role of long-term memory in learning and the importance of prior learning;

- considered the role of 'cues' in the process of remembering and the role of forgetting in learning.

THE ROLE OF ATTENTION IN LEARNING

What are you attending to at the moment? In order to think about that question, you will have had to attend to the question on the page, but there are countless other stimuli (e.g. sights, sounds, smells, etc.) that you could have been attending to.

In order to learn something, we have to attend to it. However, our attention is not entirely under our voluntary control. If there was a sudden noise outside, you'd likely find your attention drawn away from this text. Likewise, if a bee bumbles its way into your classroom, your pupils will likely find their attention drawn away from the lesson, however brilliant your teaching might be!

Some people may claim to be great multitaskers, but the evidence suggests that switching between different tasks tends to lead to a decline in our performance. It turns out the ability to multitask well is a bit of a myth (Kirschner and De Bruyckere, 2017). Switching our attention between tasks involves splitting our attentional resources; tasks typically take longer than they would individually, or the number of errors we make increases. Therefore, where we can, looking to reduce the range of distractions in the environment can help our pupils to focus their attention where we want it: on the learning.

However, pupils also have to work out what to attend to. The way we present new information to pupils can inadvertently bombard them with things to attend to. For example, imagine you're teaching some pupils with little prior knowledge about the forces acting on an aeroplane (see Figure 4.1). You present a picture of an aircraft with some arrows of different sizes pointing away (representing forces) in different directions. Which aspect of this should they be attending to? The number of arrows? The direction of the arrows? What the arrows represent? The size of the arrows? The labels for the arrows? It may seem simple to you, the teacher, that the difference in the size of the forces labelled B and D will influence the change in speed of the aeroplane. But how do your pupils know which are the most important and relevant parts to attend to? Worse still, the labels are presented separately, requiring the pupils to switch their attention between the diagram and the key to make sense of what's going on.

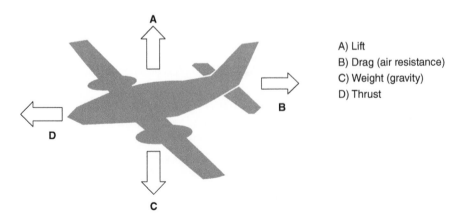

A) Lift
B) Drag (air resistance)
C) Weight (gravity)
D) Thrust

Figure 4.1   A diagram of forces acting on an aircraft

WORKING MEMORY

Assuming pupils attend to the relevant information, they then have to be able to process – or meaningfully think about – that information. Psychologists refer to the component of memory involved in conscious thinking as 'working memory'.

Working memory represents the immediate or active component of memory. Whenever we are consciously and effortfully thinking about something, we are using our working memories. For example, if I gave you a phone number and you didn't have a pen, you'd use working memory to hold on to it for the moments it took to locate a pen and paper.

Pupils rely on working memory when learning in school, whether doing mental arithmetic, reading a sentence in a book, following a teacher's explanation, or reasoning through a problem. Working memory capacity varies by individual and develops at different rates over early childhood; according to Gathercole and Alloway (2007), in a class of 30 children aged 7–8 years old, three of them might have the capacity of an average 4-year-old and three others the capacity of an average 11-year-old. However, for all of us – adults and pupils – working memory represents a 'bottleneck' to learning because it has a limited capacity and duration.

The duration of working memory is very short – within seconds to a few minutes, the information will be lost. The capacity of working memory is described by psychologists as being around four 'chunks' of information (Cowan, 2001). To illustrate this idea of a 'chunk', try a quick test that will rely on your working memory.

In this first test, give yourself ten seconds to read the letters below, then cover them up and see how many you can recall (in the right order):

BTC VBI ACP KDI OGB CTP

There are a couple of strategies you could have tried. You might have tried to mentally say the letters to yourself. Alternatively, perhaps you tried a mnemonic technique, seeing if the letters reminded you of something. Either way, the limited capacity and duration of working memory mean that most people will fail to recall all the letters (assuming they didn't cheat!).

Let's compare this with the same letters, but rearranged into 'chunks' to help your working memory. Try the task again – give yourself ten seconds, then cover them up and try to recall all the letters in the right order.

BBC ITV CIA KGB DOC PPT

Most people find this task much easier. Prior knowledge hopefully allowed your working memory to treat groups of letters as a single 'chunk'. So rather than recalling the individual letters B, B and C, you just thought 'BBC'. Furthermore, BBC and ITV are related together (TV channels), so there's a good chance that if you remember one, you'll recall the other. Similarly, CIA and KGB are related (spy agencies), as are DOC and PPT (types of computer files). From 18 individual letters, prior knowledge in long-term memory organised these into a few 'chunks' of information – much easier to hold in working memory. We'll look at long-term memory in more detail in the next section.

COGNITIVE LOAD

When we're teaching, we make demands of pupils' working memory – we want them to think hard about the new learning – which some psychologists call 'cognitive load'. In the absence of prior knowledge, working memory can be easily 'overloaded' (as you may have found in the first working memory task). The limitations of working memory have been argued to have a number of important implications for how we teach (Kirschner et al., 2006). 'Cognitive load theory' represents an attempt to encompass and explain these implications and provide a framework for developing approaches to teaching that are sympathetic to the limitations of working memory (CESE, 2017).

We can help manage the 'load' we put on pupils' working memories by carefully managing distractions, both in the environment of the classroom and the way we approach the teaching of the topic. For example, I could reduce attention-splitting by putting the labels within the diagram in Figure 4.1. We can also help to manage that 'load' by ensuring pupils have the prior knowledge that will help and considering carefully how much new content we want them to think about at once. For example, where a topic involves many new ideas, new vocabulary or complex concepts, we might helpfully manage the load on working memory by breaking the topic down into smaller steps with worked examples, before gradually reducing that scaffold, such as by providing partially worked examples that pupils complete (CESE, 2018).

KEY QUESTIONS

- Why is it important for you to assess pupils' prior knowledge before introducing new content?
- If you find that pupils' prior knowledge is much weaker than you expected, what should you consider doing next?

LONG-TERM MEMORY

Long-term memory refers to the store of experiences, life events and information that we've encountered across our lives. It forms the basis of what we know about the world, but also forms the basis of what we know about ourselves, our culture and identity, and our beliefs and attitudes.

It's called 'long-term' memory to distinguish it from 'working memory', which has very limited capacity and duration. Psychologists simply don't know the upper limit of how much information we can accumulate in long-term memory – it's practically unlimited.

Long-term memory isn't a passive form of storage like files in a filing cabinet; it actively helps us when we try to learn new things, solve complex problems, tackle new challenges and think critically (Willingham, 2009). The more knowledge we have organised in long-term memory, the easier we learn new things related to and extending that knowledge. Therefore, the knowledge and skills pupils possess in long-term memory provides a vital foundation for future learning as they encounter progressively more complex ideas over the course of their time in school.

TYPES OF LONG-TERM MEMORY

Long-term memory holds different kinds of information, and a major distinction is whether those memories are declarative ('knowing that') or non-declarative ('knowing how') (Roediger et al., 2002). Within declarative memory, there is a distinction between what psychologists call 'episodic' and 'semantic' memory:

- *Episodic memory*: Autobiographical memory for the events in our lives (e.g. What were you doing yesterday? Last year? Ten years ago?).

- *Semantic memory*: The vocabulary, knowledge and cultural ideas that help us to understand our world (e.g. What happened in 1066? Where is the country of Bolivia? How does a star like our sun form?).

Semantic memory is the ability to recall facts, meanings and concepts independent of the situation or event in which we learnt them, whereas episodic memory is the ability to reconstruct the events of our lives with reference to the time, place and emotional context of these events (Tulving, 1972). It's possible that new learning may start as episodic memory, but repeated experience leads learning to become 'decontextualised' – become independent of the time and context in which we learnt it – in the form of semantic memory (Roediger et al., 2002).

An example of non-declarative memory is procedural memory (Roediger et al., 2002), skills we've learnt through practice (e.g. how to ride a bike, how to swim).

As teachers, we're often concerned about helping our pupils develop semantic memory and procedural memory for the knowledge and skills that form the curriculum we teach.

SCHEMA AND THE IMPORTANCE OF PRIOR KNOWLEDGE

Psychologists often use the term 'schema' (pl. schemas or schemata) to describe the way long-term memory is organised. A schema can be thought of as a framework or high-level knowledge structure that helps us to organise and interpret new information and experiences (Roediger et al., 2002). For example, when you saw the letters 'BBC' and 'ITV' in the working memory task above, you were able to benefit from the organisation of knowledge – your schema – in long-term memory. The letters B, B and C have strong internal associations, and BBC and ITV together are likely to have a strong association. Therefore, if you recalled one of them, there was a fair chance you'd recall the other. Prior knowledge actively supports new learning, and teachers can help pupils by explicitly linking new learning to knowledge and experiences they already possess. This can help pupils to integrate new learning with the 'schemas' they already have.

However, it's also important to recognise that pupils come to our lessons with prior knowledge that can be potentially unhelpful to their learning. Where pupils' prior knowledge might include misconceptions, stereotypes or common misunderstandings, it is likely to make it harder to integrate new learning with those pre-existing schemas. This means that we need to think carefully about how we sequence the introduction of new material. Where their prior knowledge of a topic is very limited or we introduce new ideas too quickly, there's a chance that any prior misconceptions will continue to influence their thinking. We can think of prior learning as the foundation for future learning, so it's important to help pupils in developing secure knowledge and understanding of more basic ideas before introducing more complex ones.

KEY QUESTIONS

- Thinking about your own prior knowledge about learning, what have you encountered so far that is new or different to what you previously believed?

- Why is it important for teachers to assess for misconceptions?

REMEMBERING AND FORGETTING

Remembering involves retrieving information from long-term memory. Whenever you learn something, elements of the context in which you learnt the material are stored along with that information (Tulving and Thompson, 1973). These aspects of the context then act as what psychologists call 'cues' for the future retrieval of memories stored in long-term memory, making them available to working memory and conscious awareness. For example, if I ask you, 'What is the capital city of France?' you have to engage in a 'mental search' of long-term memory to find the answer (likely an effortless search in this case). Elements of the question (capital city, France) act as 'cues' which guide that mental search.

Which elements of the context are stored when we form new memories? It will be influenced by what we were attending to and can be somewhat unpredictable. For example, in a lesson on forces, hopefully some of the context your pupils store will involve relevant and useful cues for retrieving that knowledge later (e.g. balanced and unbalanced forces, changes in speed or direction, Newtons as units of force); however, less relevant aspects of the context are also likely to be stored, depending on what the pupil was attending to (e.g. the type of aeroplane used in the diagram (Figure 4.1), which classroom you were in, the ink colour used to write the labels, etc.).

One of the difficulties in remembering is that those cues provide the guide to our mental searches, and in the absence of those cues we're much less likely to bring the right information to mind. For example, if you've only ever used aeroplanes in your examples, will pupils successfully retrieve information about forces when they see a question about submarines? Fortunately, our long-term memories are not static. Each time a memory is retrieved from long-term memory, that memory is changed, potentially adding to or altering the cues associated with that memory and making that knowledge easier to retrieve again in the future (Karpicke, 2012).

When thinking about learning, it's also important to remember about forgetting! When we learn new things, we might recall them readily over the course of the lesson, but the strength of that understanding in long-term memory will likely be quite weak, and we rapidly forget what we've learnt (Bjork and Bjork, 1992). When teaching a new topic, it's possible that your pupils will forget most of the details of that lesson by the time you next see them. However, the good news is that the learning wasn't wasted. Each time pupils revisit that material, they'll relearn it quicker and retain it for longer. In fact, forgetting (a bit) is a useful part of learning. If we revisit materials while they are still 'fresh in mind', the benefits tend to be much less than if we allow some time for forgetting before returning to the topic (Bjork and Bjork, 1992).

Therefore, it's important to plan spaced opportunities for pupils to retrieve knowledge and practise skills to help consolidate memory. For example, the details of a lesson on forces will likely be forgotten quite quickly, the rate and extent likely influenced by how much prior knowledge the pupils possessed and how complex or abstract the ideas were. Providing some time for pupils to forget and then quizzing them on the topic can help to strengthen the memory for the material (Agarwal et al., 2018). Where pupils are quite successful at recalling the topic, you can make it harder by increasing the spacing. On the other hand, if they aren't able to recall the material, you might reduce the amount of time before quizzing them again, or consider reteaching some part of the material if their understanding is weak or there appear to be misconceptions creeping back in.

KEY QUESTIONS

- Why might it be important to vary the questions you ask when teaching? What might happen if you always asked the same question in the same way about a topic?

- Why is the opportunity to revisit and recall previously learnt material within the curriculum you teach potentially so important for pupils when they move to the next stage of their education (e.g. moving up to primary school, secondary school, further education or higher education)?

CONCLUSION

This chapter has explored the role of memory within the process of learning and explored a 'simple model' of how human memory works, which will help support you with section 2 of the ECF. Understanding the role of memory within learning can be helpful when thinking about your teaching and your pupils' experience in lessons, but it's important to understand that this is a simplification – learning is a complex process (teaching doubly so!). There are many elements required for learning that haven't been discussed here. For example, this chapter explored the role of working memory and the idea that it can become 'overloaded' by distractions or by the way we present new material. But using working memory requires effort, and engaging in effortful thinking requires motivation. However, understanding some of the aspects of memory that influence pupil learning can provide a useful starting point as you work to develop your teaching.

KEY CONCEPTS AND FURTHER READING

RETRIEVAL PRACTICE

Agarwal, P.K., Roediger, H.L., McDaniel, M.A. and McDermott, K.B. (2018) *How to Use Retrieval Practice to Improve Learning*. Available at: http://pdf.retrievalpractice.org/RetrievalPracticeGuide.pdf

- This guide explains the research underpinning retrieval practice and how it can be used as a strategy to improve learning.

COGNITIVE LOAD THEORY

Centre for Education Statistics and Evaluation (CESE) (2017) *Cognitive Load Theory: Research That Teachers Really Need to Understand*. Available at: www.cese.nsw.gov.au//images/stories/PDF/cognitive-load-theory-VR_AA3.pdf

- This literature review provides a helpful overview of cognitive load theory and offers recommendations for the classroom.

Centre for Education Statistics and Evaluation (CESE) (2018) *Cognitive Load Theory in Practice: Examples for the Classroom*. Available at: www.cese.nsw.gov.au//images/stories/PDF/Cognitive_load_theory_practice_guide_AA.pdf

- Building on the literature review, this resource outlines seven teaching strategies that emerge from cognitive load theory.

WORKING MEMORY

Gathercole, S.E. and Alloway, T. (2007) *Understanding Working Memory: A Classroom Guide*. Available at: www.mrc-cbu.cam.ac.uk/wp-content/uploads/2013/01/WM-classroom-guide.pdf

- This booklet provides an introduction to working memory and the role it plays in supporting learning.

Willingham, D. (2009) Why don't students like school? Because the mind is not designed for thinking. *American Educator*, 33(1): 4–13.

- This article is an excerpt from Willingham's book of the same title – page 7 of this article includes a really helpful, simple model of the mind.

━━━━ REFERENCES ━━━━

Agarwal, P.K., Roediger, H.L., McDaniel, M.A. and McDermott, K.B. (2018) *How to Use Retrieval Practice to Improve Learning*. Available at: http://pdf.retrievalpractice.org/RetrievalPracticeGuide.pdf

American Psychological Association (APA) (2018) *APA Dictionary of Psychology: Learning*. Available at: https://dictionary.apa.org/learning

Bjork, R.A. and Bjork, E.L. (1992) A new theory of disuse and an old theory of stimulus fluctuation. In A. Healy, S. Kosslyn and R. Shiffrin (eds), *From Learning Processes to Cognitive Processes: Essays in Honor of William K. Estes, Vol. 2.* Hillsdale, NJ: Lawrence Erlbaum, pp35–67.

Centre for Education Statistics and Evaluation (CESE) (2017) *Cognitive Load Theory: Research That Teachers Really Need to Understand.* Available at: www.cese.nsw.gov.au//images/stories/PDF/cognitive-load-theory-VR_AA3.pdf

Centre for Education Statistics and Evaluation (CESE) (2018) *Cognitive Load Theory in Practice: Examples for the Classroom.* Available at: www.cese.nsw.gov.au//images/stories/PDF/Cognitive_load_theory_practice_guide_AA.pdf

Cowan, N. (2001) The magical number 4 in short-term memory: a reconsideration of mental storage capacity. *Behavioral and Brain Sciences*, 24(1): 87–114.

Gathercole, S.E. and Alloway, T. (2007) *Understanding Working Memory: A Classroom Guide.* Available at: www.mrc-cbu.cam.ac.uk/wp-content/uploads/2013/01/WM-classroom-guide.pdf

Karpicke, J.D. (2012) Retrieval-based learning: active retrieval promotes meaningful learning. *Current Directions in Psychological Science*, 21(3): 157–63.

Kirschner, P.A. and De Bruyckere, P. (2017) The myths of the digital native and the multitasker. *Teaching and Teacher Education*, 67(1): 135–42.

Kirschner, P.A., Sweller, J. and Clark, R.E. (2006) Why minimal guidance during instruction does not work: an analysis of the failure of constructivist, discovery, problem-based, experiential, and inquiry-based teaching. *Educational Psychologist*, 41(2): 75–86.

Roediger, H.L. III, Marsh, E.J. and Lee, S.C. (2002) Kinds of memory. In H. Pashler and D. Medin (eds), *Stevens' Handbook of Experimental Psychology: Memory and Cognitive Processes.* New York: John Wiley & Sons, pp1–41.

Tulving, E. (1972) Episodic and semantic memory. In E. Tulving and W. Donaldson (eds), *Organization of Memory.* New York: Academic Press, pp381–403.

Tulving, E. and Thomson, D.M. (1973) Encoding specificity and retrieval processes in episodic memory. *Psychological Review*, 80(5): 352–73.

Willingham, D. (2009) Why don't students like school? Because the mind is not designed for thinking. *American Educator*, 33(1): 4–13.

5

MEMORIES THAT STICK

NASIMA RIAZAT

CURRICULUM LEAD, PENDLE VALE COLLEGE, LANCASHIRE, UK

JONATHAN FIRTH

SCHOOL OF EDUCATION, UNIVERSITY OF STRATHCLYDE, GLASGOW, UK

INTRODUCTION

We all want to ensure that our efforts in teaching and learning are supporting students well both for assessments and for everyday life. This chapter explains several evidence-based strategies to ensure new concepts are stored in your students' long-term memory so that they can use this knowledge flexibly and creatively. Building these strategies into your teaching practice will support learners to remember, understand and apply the content from your lessons, as well as modelling good independent study habits.

> ### CHAPTER OBJECTIVES
>
> This chapter will help you to understand:
>
> - how the design and teaching order of learning and revision tasks can be made more efficient;
> - effective ways to consolidate new learning into long-term memory;
> - how to ensure factual knowledge is linked to higher-order thinking skills to deepen learning.

THE DESIGN AND ORDER OF LEARNING AND REVISION TASKS
SPACING AND INTERLEAVING: WHAT IS THE SPACING EFFECT?

How should you schedule learning activities for students? Consider whether you agree with the following statement:

Learners should practise what they have studied immediately, because letting time pass will mean they are more likely to gradually forget this learning.

It's common for schools to schedule initial learning and follow-up practice tasks quite close together. You may teach a new topic and then do a short review, or cover a topic one week and set homework on it for the following weekend.

However, opportunities for your students to practise and retrieve are most effective when spaced out with long delays in between (Rawson and Dunlosky, 2011). This is called the *spacing effect*. Therefore, the best evidence-based response to the above statement would be to disagree!

KEY IDEAS

Points to be aware of when using the spacing effect include the following:

- Consider returning to topics after a delay rather than covering them once (e.g. delay homework and practice activities).

- Schedule topics so that they are spaced out over a number of weeks for regular, repeated practice.

- Project and practical work could be designed to mix older topics with your current one, as doing so will naturally space out practice.

- Teach your students that long study sessions are best replaced by multiple short ones.

Overall, the idea that a delay is unhelpful should be challenged; instead, delays allow students to retrieve their learning and deepen it.

WHY DOES SPACING HELP?

At times consolidation of learning may appear unnecessary. Perhaps your learners have been getting answers right in class, or they have correctly completed an in-class quiz or exit pass. It is tempting under these circumstances for you to conclude that the only consolidation required is some pre-exam revision.

However, classroom performance can be more short-lived than we might think. Even when we see confident, accurate answering in the classroom, this doesn't mean that new concepts and skills have been properly consolidated as deep, permanent learning.

Students are more likely to forget immediately after studying; Ebbinghaus's classic 1885 'forgetting curve' shows that forgetting is rapid at first but then slows down (Ebbinghaus, 1964).

Consider the following:

- If concepts are studied intensively over five lessons in week 1, with a short test in week 10, then learners will experience nine weeks of forgetting between initial study and the test itself in week 10.

to a virus. This task could be lagged to space out previous learning (e.g. the immune system) rather than focusing on a current topic.

As well as prompting retrieval, such techniques prompt learners to think carefully about how the learning fits together and to check their own knowledge.

HIGHER-ORDER THINKING SKILLS

If it seems that we are calling for a major focus on low-level factual recall, don't worry. Facts are important, but so is higher-order thinking! And it's vitally important for the two to interlink.

There are techniques that can help with this too:

- *Elaborative retrieval* means retrieving information in a way that involves expanding on initial learning by adding more detail. One simple classroom strategy for this is the use of a spider diagram, through which more information can gradually be added to a basic outline.

- *Thinking of examples.* Focusing on the skill of application, ask learners to think of real-world examples or uses of concepts that they have learnt. This could be done as a homework task, though it is best if the teacher checks that examples are accurate (Zamary et al., 2016).

- *Interrogative questioning* involves frequently asking 'why' rather than just accepting new learning as facts. This helps to promote deeper thinking and to strengthen the links among previous learning, and the curiosity it promotes helps to strengthen long-term memory. For example, using the example of the suffragettes, we could ask students, 'Why did they chain themselves to the Houses of Parliament? Why not to their own front doors? Why did they use chains and not rope? Why did they go on hunger strike?' And so on.

- *Dual coding* involves combining visuals and text to make the information entering long-term memory richer and easier to recall (Clark and Paivio, 1991). It means that learners have two memory traces (visual and verbal) that they can retrieve, therefore acting as a form of scaffolding. Think about how to incorporate dual coding when supporting students to take notes during a lesson.

It's best to teach these strategies explicitly to your students in the classroom to enable learners to use them confidently and effectively in their independent study and revision time too.

USING THE STRATEGIES FOR INDEPENDENT LEARNING

Clearly, any study strategy used for independent study and revision has to be straightforward and not too demanding in terms of the resources required. One of the simplest ways to introduce retrieval practice is to include an instruction at the foot of a page of notes, along the lines of, 'Now close the booklet and write down everything you can remember'.

Learners can also be prompted to create their own revision materials in class time. In general, flash cards are a great revision resource, ideal for retrieval practice; however, it is worth taking time to ensure that students are using the flash cards effectively (Seggie and Riazat, 2018). For example, the lesson plenary could be devoted to creating revision flash cards that include both visual and verbal prompts, making use of dual coding.

Agarwal and Bain (2019) suggest the following principles when revising with flash cards:

- *No cheating*. Ensure that learners are testing themselves, not just looking at the answers.

- *Reorder*. Shuffle the cards in order to gain the benefit of interleaving.

- *Repeat*. Learners should put cards aside once they have initially mastered them, but return to them at least three times after a delay. They may be surprised how badly they do, but this just shows why spaced practice is useful!

For material where the order and context are vital, a gap-fill task can serve a similar purpose. Quizzing apps and websites such as Quizlet or Sporcle are excellent for retrieval that involves visual materials. Music, cooking, and sports practice often involve retrieval without the need for flash cards.

'Lagged' homework, which focuses at least partly on older topics, can also prompt useful retrieval. For example, rather than summarising the required information for a project task, ask learners to retrieve it from memory, and then check their notes/textbooks to ensure that they got it right. In one of Jonathan's previous schools, pupils were asked to explain concepts to a family member as 'talking homework', prompting retrieval and elaboration.

CONCLUSION

This chapter set out to explore how to deepen and consolidate new learning. The strategies that we have explained will make your teaching more effective so that students can recall what they need for tests and in everyday life. They will also support students to become more effective independent learners. And fundamentally, such strategies are very simple to use.

KEY QUESTIONS

- What small changes can you make to your current practice to allow students to think about studying more effectively?

- What opportunities can you take to model effective revision strategies for students to emulate when learning or revising independently?

- How can you teach students to space their learning and decide what needs to be revisited more than once?

KEY CONCEPTS AND FURTHER READING

RETRIEVAL PRACTICE THROUGH EVERYDAY CLASSROOM ACTIVITIES

Agarwal, P.K. and Bain, P. (2019) *Powerful Teaching: Unleash the Science of Learning*. New York: Jossey-Bass.

- This book has lots of detail on how to implement retrieval practice through everyday classroom activities, and also covers spacing, interleaving, elaboration and other techniques. It explains much of the science behind the techniques too.

DESIRABLE DIFFICULTIES

Bjork, E.L. and Bjork, R.A. (2011) Making things hard on yourself, but in a good way: creating desirable difficulties to enhance learning. In M.A. Gernsbacher, R.W. Pew, L.M. Hough and J.R. Pomeranz (eds), *Psychology and the Real World: Essays Illustrating Fundamental Contributions to Society*. New York: Worth Publishers, pp56–64.

- This chapter sets out the idea of desirable difficulties – including spacing and interleaving – in a very accessible way and covers the difference between learning and performance. It is available open access online.

SPACED PRACTICE

Seggie, J. and Riazat, N. (2018) Retrieval practice in practice: using revision cards to change student misconceptions about how and when to revise. *Impact*, 3: 53.

- This article explains how to embed the practice of students revising regularly and frequently, rather than just before their exam or test, and explores how to create meaningful revision cards with students.

INDEPENDENT LEARNING

Smith, M. and Firth, J. (2018) *Psychology in the Classroom: A Teacher's Guide to What Works*. London: Routledge.

- This book covers a range of psychological principles from memory to motivation, explaining how they can inform lesson planning and teaching techniques. Chapter 8 focuses on implementing successful independent learning in school pupils.

REFERENCES

Agarwal, P.K. and Bain, P. (2019) *Powerful Teaching: Unleash the Science of Learning*. New York: Jossey-Bass.

Agarwal, P.K., D'Antonio, L., Roediger, H.L., McDermott, K.B. and McDaniel, M.A. (2014) Classroom-based programs of retrieval practice reduce middle school and high school students' test anxiety. *Journal of Applied Research in Memory and Cognition*, 3(3): 131–9.

Bjork, E.L. and Bjork, R.A. (2011) Making things hard on yourself, but in a good way: creating desirable difficulties to enhance learning. In M.A. Gernsbacher, R.W. Pew, L.M. Hough and J.R. Pomeranz (eds), *Psychology and the Real World: Essays Illustrating Fundamental Contributions to Society*. New York: Worth Publishers, pp56–64.

Clark, J.M. and Paivio, A. (1991) Dual coding theory and education. *Educational Psychology Review*, 3(3): 149–210.

Ebbinghaus, H. (1964) *Memory: A Contribution to Experimental Psychology* (H.A. Ruger and C.E. Bussenius, trans.). New York: Dover. (Original work published 1885).

Koh, A.W.L., Lee, S.C. and Lim, S.W.H. (2018) The learning benefits of teaching: a retrieval practice hypothesis. *Applied Cognitive Psychology*, 32(3): 401–10.

Rawson, K.A. and Dunlosky, J. (2011) Optimizing schedules of retrieval practice for durable and efficient learning: how much is enough? *Journal of Experimental Psychology: General*, 140(3): 283–302.

Seggie, J. and Riazat, N. (2018) Retrieval practice in practice: using revision cards to change student misconceptions about how and when to revise. *Impact*, 3: 53.

Smith, M. and Firth, J. (2018) *Psychology in the Classroom: A Teacher's Guide to What Works*. London: Routledge.

Zamary, A., Rawson, K.A. and Dunlosky, J. (2016) How accurately can students evaluate the quality of self-generated examples of declarative concepts? Not well, and feedback does not help. *Learning and Instruction*, 46: 12–20.

6

BUILDING UNDERSTANDING

PRITESH RAICHURA

HEAD OF SCIENCE, MICHAELA COMMUNITY SCHOOL, GREATER LONDON, UK

INTRODUCTION

If 'memory is the residue of thought' (Willingham, 2009), then teachers have a duty to ensure students are constantly thinking about the content of their subjects in their lessons. Activities planned by teachers must pass the test, 'Does this activity maximise the amount of time my students spend thinking about the content I want them to remember?' A role play to teach the structure of the atom probably requires students to think more about who will play which role than about the structure of the atom. In contrast, a clear, explicit explanation given by a teacher using a simple diagram, interspersed with lots of questions, is very likely to result in rapid student learning.

If we measure how time is spent in the most effective lessons, there are three categories of activities that ensure students are thinking about the intended content and making significant learning gains: teacher explanation, student practice (verbal and written) and feedback (Rosenshine, 2012).

Section 4 of the Early Career Framework (ECF) concerns planning well-structured lessons. This involves learning to design a sequence of lessons that builds understanding of the concepts on the curriculum. To achieve this, your *explanations* need to be clear enough for all of your students to follow. Second, your lesson sequence must give students the opportunity to *practise* until they can demonstrate fluency without your help. Third, during both the explanation and practice stages, you must constantly do two things: gather information about how well your students are understanding the content *and* correct their mistakes and misconceptions. In other words, you are both *collecting* feedback about how your students are doing and *giving* corrective feedback to make up for any deficits in your initial explanation.

HOW TO SEQUENCE IDEAS

Before you start to plan a unit of lessons, ensure that your subject knowledge for the entire topic is secure. If you begin teaching a unit but your knowledge of content later in the sequence is patchy, you will miss opportunities to plan effectively.

CHAPTER OBJECTIVES

In this chapter, you will learn:

- how to sequence ideas:
    - building on prior learning;
    - organising ideas to build understanding;

- how to break down ideas into constituent parts:
    - lesson versus idea;
    - atomisation;

- how to deliver clear explanations:
    - examples and non-examples;
    - dual coding;
    - modelling;

- how to check pupils are following an explanation:
    - five questioning techniques;
    - choosing techniques strategically;

- how to plan student practice:
    - writing practice questions;
    - guidance fading.

Before you find out exactly what background knowledge your students have in reality, you need to establish what you would expect your students to already have mastered before it is even possible for you to move on to the content you intend to teach. For example, if you were teaching a class about natural selection, it would be essential for your pupils to know examples of adaptations, and have a firm understanding of competition, variation and inheritance. Without firm knowledge of these ideas, natural selection will be impossible to understand. Your first step to sequencing lessons should be to write down exactly what you expect students to know about each of these concepts. For example, focusing on competition, can they successfully explain that:

- organisms only compete when resources are limited;

- in the wild, population sizes usually keep on rising until resources become limited and cause competition;

- animals compete for food, territory and mates (e.g. tigers compete for deer, goldfinches for nest sites, male elephant seals for females);

- many animals fight each other for these limited resources;

- plants compete for light, water and space;

- if organisms fail to compete for these, they will either die or fail to reproduce.

Notice how specific this list is. If you do not have 100 per cent clarity about the precise knowledge, definitions and even examples you expect your students to know, then you will not be able to help them commit this knowledge to long-term memory.

You can plan your first lesson(s) around asking questions to ensure this knowledge is secure. If it is, you can proceed with your teaching sequence. If your students are struggling, then you will need to plan review lessons. Failing to check this knowledge is akin to building on foundations of sand: your attempts at teaching new knowledge will fail.

Next, for the unit you are planning on teaching, write a list of all the main concepts and pieces of knowledge that you want your students to master. This might come from a centralised curriculum, the specification of the course you are teaching, from a textbook, or from your head of department. These need to be concrete bits of knowledge, not generic skills. You cannot teach a skill in a vacuum of knowledge (Christodoulou, 2014).

Now start to play around with a sequence for these key bits of knowledge. There may be more than one optimal sequence. The underlying idea is to produce a sequence that will best build understanding. In large, this comes from having excellent subject knowledge to inform your decisions. Your guiding principles are as follows:

1. Some knowledge must precede other knowledge for it to make any sense at all. For example, melting and boiling points cannot make sense if you do not teach students what solids, liquids and gases are. This is the most important sequencing principle.

2. Concrete ideas should generally precede abstract ones because you cannot think about abstract ideas without concrete examples to refer to. For example, you cannot teach students that 'competition occurs when there are limited resources' if they cannot anchor that knowledge to an example, such as lots of foxes competing for a few rabbits to eat.

3. Build on prior learning. It is helpful to anchor new knowledge to existing knowledge.

Once you have your ideas in order, you are ready to start dividing them up into lessons.

HOW TO BREAK DOWN IDEAS INTO CONSTITUENT PARTS

The trick with planning lessons is not to see individual lessons as segments of time in which equal amounts of learning take place. If you have planned a sequence of ten lessons and know what you expect your students to have understood and practised by the *end* of the sequence, then it does not matter exactly how much you cover in a single lesson. For some topics, you might spend a whole lesson modelling and questioning. While this means pupils do get lots of opportunity to practise, it occurs only in short, sharp bursts. Your goal here is to build understanding, not fluency. Then the whole next lesson might be big chunks of independent practice and feedback. Here, you will be building fluency and tackling misconceptions. A common belief is to think,

'But every lesson must contain a starter, a main activity and a plenary'. Unless this is your school policy, I would recommend focusing on the destination to be reached at the final lesson in the sequence and see the journey up until there as an irregular one, dictated by the content you are teaching, rather than being dictated by a fixed lesson structure.

Break up your sequence into roughly what you expect to cover over the number of lessons specified by your department's timeline. Each idea then needs to be 'atomised'. This means breaking down an idea into the greatest number of smaller ideas/steps that you possibly can. Some examples in maths (Boulton, 2017) and chemistry (Raichura, 2018) are referenced. The trick to good atomisation is to make *everything* explicit. Have you explained every single idea necessary for the main idea to make sense?

Another example: if you are atomising an explanation of electrical current, defining it as the 'rate of flow of charge' is not sufficient. Do you intend to explain what rate means? What is a charge? What does it mean for a charge to flow? Continually interrogate whether you have made all ideas explicit. Methods of interrogation include:

- defining all words that students may not have been explicitly taught before;

- identifying every relevant step between a cause and its effect, or within a chronology;

- for procedures (e.g. calculations, science practical methods, using a paintbrush), making every step so explicit that the procedure could be followed by a complete novice.

It is these 'atomised' ideas that will form the basis of planning your explanations, practice and feedback for each lesson.

KEY QUESTIONS

Pick a topic that you are planning lessons for:

- Can you specify the prior knowledge you expect your students to have mastered already?

- Can you specify the new knowledge that you intend your students to learn?

- Can you sequence the knowledge to use the principles in the first section?

- Can you atomise the first idea in the sequence using the methods of interrogation in the second section?

HOW TO PLAN A CLEAR EXPLANATION

Scripting an explanation is a useful way to plan it. Sharing this model explanation with pupils to read and annotate together can serve as an accessible reference point for students when completing independent practice. It also serves as an exemplar for the type of subject-specific language you use. To make your explanations as clear as possible, the first rule is to never start an explanation with an abstract idea. Instead, begin with concrete examples that illustrate the abstract idea. For example, write about sweating to cool down and shivering to warm up when explaining the principle of homeostasis. By doing this, when the abstract definition of homeostasis (maintenance of a constant internal environment) is shared *after* the examples, then the phrase 'internal environment' will suddenly have meaning. In this instance, students can understand 'internal environment' to mean 'temperature'. What makes concrete examples so useful, then, is that they give pupils something to think about when they encounter the generalised definition.

DUAL CODING

It is very hard to follow a verbal (or written) explanation if there is a lot of new content and vocabulary. This is because our working memories, which process information from our environments, are limited in their capacity (Cowan, 2010). By the time we hear the third new word, we will have forgotten the first two and their examples. The solution to this is to draw diagrams or write down bullet points as you deliver your explanation. This relieves your students of the burden of remembering those ideas in addition to listening to your explanation. The use of a visual to accompany a text or a verbal explanation is called dual coding. Since our brains process visual and verbal information separately, dual coding increases the amount of information we can hold in our working memory, cleverly bypassing its limitations (Clark and Paivio, 1991).

Dual coding is most easily done on a whiteboard, but a visualiser (a camera that projects what you write in an exercise book on to the board) has two main benefits. First, it allows you to face your students, which is better for engagement and behaviour. Second, it allows you to reveal pre-drawn or printed diagrams/lists that you can annotate live. Doing this in blank exercise books allows you to revisit previous diagrams and annotations for revision, re-explanation and retrieval practice in the future.

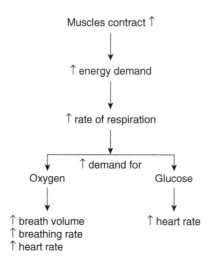

Figure 6.1   The effects of exercise on the body are explained using a flow chart

At its simplest, your diagram can be a few words with some arrows to show the relationship between them, revealed or written one step at a time (see Figure 6.1). This is incredibly helpful because it means students do not have to hold the words in their working memory and can instead pay attention to the relationship between the words that are already present on the page by assigning meaning to the arrows. While your ultimate goal as a teacher is for the students to eventually commit the words, their meanings, and relationships between the words to memory, during the explanation stage your goal is to create understanding.

Simple drawings depicting the thing you are talking about can relieve your students' working memories while they focus on the additional information. The example explanation below is about how deforestation increases the amount of carbon dioxide in the atmosphere. Read the explanation without looking at Figure 6.2 below:

Living plants absorb carbon dioxide from the atmosphere during photosynthesis. This helps them to grow. The carbon from the carbon dioxide is stored in the plant during photosynthesis. So, photosynthesis removes carbon from the atmosphere and the carbon is stored up in the plant. However, when trees are cut down during deforestation, the trees stop photosynthesising. Not only do they stop removing carbon dioxide from the atmosphere, but all of the stored carbon is released again as the tree decays.

This is an excellent explanation, but it is very tricky for a novice to follow because by the time you reach the final sentence, it is likely that the students listening will have forgotten what was said earlier. Now consider the explanation again, but this time look at Figure 6.2. Drawing a tree and showing it takes in carbon dioxide one step at a time immediately relieves students of the burden of that fact. They can then focus on the rest of the explanation. In this way, the diagram helps students to build understanding by ensuring they follow the explanation.

An obvious case when dual coding is helpful is when you are describing structures that students need to imagine; they are far easier to understand through a diagram, where relative positions of different parts of an object can be seen instead of being described (e.g. if teaching about the structure of a cell, show a diagram of the cell with the most pertinent features drawn).

MODELLING

Sometimes a diagram is not useful during an explanation. Instead, you want to model how to perform a calculation or construct a sentence. Modelling well involves making every step of your thinking explicit to the students live. Modelling a calculation means showing every step of your working out to your students – known as a worked example. Modelling the construction of a sentence involves thinking out loud about your choice of words, syntax, and reference to how the sentence you are writing answers the question.

Such modelling is exceptionally useful for three reasons. First, it forces you to make every step *explicit* – this means that no student is left guessing how you transitioned from one step to the next. This is a fundamental principle of explicit instruction. Thinking out loud during modelling is key to this. Second, it forces you to come up with a consistent method that students can emulate during practice. Finally, modelling live allows you to slow down your instruction at a pace that your pupils are more likely to follow. If you use a PowerPoint presentation and click through a model answer, you risk losing your students along the way.

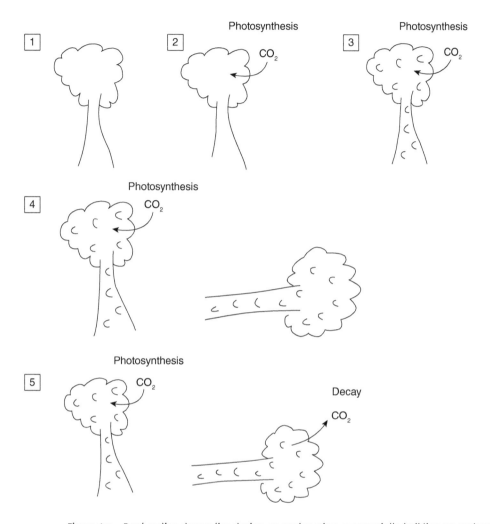

Figure 6.2   Dual coding drawn live during an explanation, sequentially building up understanding

During modelling, the teacher is doing the hard work. Although the teacher might ask students questions along the way, there is still high dependence on the teacher for understanding. After modelling, it is important to let students practise.

HOW TO CHECK PUPILS ARE FOLLOWING AN EXPLANATION

Obtaining a high success rate in the class is crucial for building motivation and therefore buy-in. Therefore, high-frequency comprehension questions are highly effective during an explanation. Such questioning also holds students accountable for listening. By being meticulous with your questioning, you ensure that every student follows you as you lead them through the explanation, building understanding incrementally. Never ask questions about topics that you have not taught the class before. You cannot expect students to know if they have not been taught, unless you have given them sufficient knowledge to deduce the answer.

It is important to ask questions in different ways. Five common questioning techniques used during explicit instruction are as follows:

1. *Hands up*: After posing a question, students who know the answer put their hands up.

2. *Cold call*: After posing a question, the teacher picks a student, regardless of whether they have their hand up or not.

3. *Choral response*: After posing a question, the teacher pauses and then gives a clear signal, after which all students in the class say the answer simultaneously.

4. *Turn to your partner (TTYP)*: Pupils are told their pairings. After posing a question, pupils tell their partner the answer, so that half the class is answering the question while the other half listens.

5. *Mini whiteboard*: After posing a question, the pupils draw/write their answer on individual whiteboards and hold their boards up for the teacher to check.

The strategy chosen can be varied as much or as little as suits your purposes. Table 6.1 summarises the advantages, disadvantages and tips for using the techniques effectively, but there are a few overarching principles that help you choose the best strategy to use in a given moment. Hands up, choral response and TTYP can all be very energising during an explanation. They can be used to inject pace and increase participation in the lesson. Cold call and mini whiteboard questions force students to think and can be very revealing of misconceptions. Listening to or reading the answers to these questions should inform your next steps. Have you unearthed a misconception that you can address? Have you realised there was a gap in your explanation that you need to fill? The most important pedagogical principle to understand here is that questioning is an inextricable part of giving explanations: your students' answers to your questions act as feedback for your explanations; the most pertinent points in your explanations should inform the questions you plan to ask.

Table 6.1 Questioning techniques

Technique	Advantage	Disadvantage	Using it effectively
Hands up	Visible gauge of which students *think* they know the answer.	Picking one volunteer gives you very limited information about how well the class as a whole has grasped/recalled an idea.	When one volunteer answers successfully, do not make the inference that the entire class has understood.
Cold call	Holds pupils accountable, especially when used frequently. Provides a valuable snapshot of understanding if the student is chosen carefully.	You only gain information about one pupil at a time.	Use simpler questions to target students who you suspect might not have been listening. Use more demanding questions to check for understanding. Choose students whose answer will inform you about how much longer you need to spend explaining an idea.

Choral response	Injects energy into the room and builds a feeling of success.	Only works for very concise answers.	Only works well if everyone says their answer at precisely the same time. So, you need to first make sure you give all pupils thinking time (pause after a question). Second, ensure you give a clear, sharp signal: '3, 2, 1!'
TTYP, followed by one of the above	Everyone has the opportunity to orally rehearse their answer, especially if you instruct partners to repeat the other partner's answer.	Potentially allows one person in each pair to be lazy and rely on their partner to do the hard thinking.	Follow TTYP answers with accountability: 'What did Anas just say?'
Mini whiteboards	Forces every student to answer the question. Every student's answer is visible simultaneously.	Can be tricky to check longer answers quickly.	Practise a slick routine for getting whiteboards out and ready, for showing the correct answer, and for wiping boards clean.

Planning challenging questions to check for understanding is important. Challenge comes in many forms, including but not limited to the following:

- Linking two or more facts together (e.g. 'What is the difference between photosynthesis and decay?').

- Applying an idea to a new context (e.g. 'Why are fossil fuels needed in aeroplanes?' when you have previously only referenced cars).

- Recalling a fact that was learnt a long time ago (e.g. 'What is a mixture?' if asked long after the definition is taught). Just because this is a recall question does not mean it is not rigorous.

- Categorising a new example (e.g. having taught regulating temperature and water levels are examples of homeostasis, 'Is regulating blood sugar level an example of homeostasis? Why or why not?').

HOW TO PLAN STUDENT PRACTICE

Planning practice is integral to lesson planning. If you plan practice for students to complete after each segment of your explanation, you will succeed in building understanding in the following ways:

- Students have the opportunity to rehearse the ideas you explained and modelled, resulting in eventual fluency.

- Collecting information about which students answered practice questions successfully gives you information about whether to move on or reteach a particular idea.

- Collecting information about students' wrong answers or flaws in the language they use allows you to react and give them feedback to help them improve. Feeding back to the whole class can help everyone benefit.

Consider solving an equation, 'Calculate the speed of a train if it covers 30 metres in 3 seconds'. To solve the equation requires some factual knowledge, such as 'speed equals distance divided by time'. But once I know that fact, I have to follow a set of procedures to get my answer: identify what the distance in the question is, identify the time, and divide the two. This example illustrates that knowledge can be categorised as being declarative or procedural (Reif, 2008). Put simply, declarative knowledge is the *what* (the facts of a subject) while procedural knowledge is the *how* (the steps involved in a particular procedure).

Knowing this is incredibly useful for designing the practice that you give to students. If you are practising a procedure, you break down the procedure into lots of steps (atomisation) and then get students to practise the steps, individually at first, and then together.

You can use partially completed worked examples that the students fill in. Eventually, practice can be given without any guidance at all. This is known as guidance fading (Renkl, 2012).

For declarative knowledge, there are lots of ways to practise the knowledge. Simple recall and comprehension questions are powerful – they force the students to think about the content and can involve retrieval practice, which is 'reconstructing knowledge by bringing it to mind from … memory' (Sumeracki and Weinstein, 2018, p13), improving learning. The bulk of initial practice can be lots of comprehension and recall questions – these are easy to write and give students lots of opportunity to embed the knowledge they need.

Diagrams are powerful tools for practice activities. Students can convert a diagram into sentences that describe or explain what the diagram depicts (for a variety of examples, see Ashbee, 2018). It can be helpful for you to write out what sentences you expect your students to be able to construct about the diagrams before the lesson. This will help you identify vocabulary that you need to make explicit, informing your initial explanation.

KEY QUESTIONS

- For the topic you atomised earlier in this chapter, can you script an explanation with concrete examples to share before the abstract idea?

- Plan a series of diagrams, models or worked examples (as suitable) that support your explanation.

- Plan a series of 15 questions that you will ask throughout your explanation. What factors will affect your choice of strategy for each question?

- Plan a series of practice questions for students to complete independently.

CONCLUSION

Planning a unit of lessons involves starting with the knowledge you expect your students to know, followed by sequencing the ideas for the unit. Good sequencing helps build understanding. A sequence can be fleshed out by atomising the main ideas. These can be taught explicitly, using concrete examples before abstract definitions, dual coding, and using lots of questioning to both hold pupils to account but also help them to check for understanding. Collecting information about what your students understand informs your subsequent explanations, which complete the feedback loop. Planning good practice for students requires you to identify whether the knowledge you are teaching is declarative or procedural. Guidance fading using a series of worked examples works well for procedural knowledge, whereas comprehension and retrieval questions are good activities for practising declarative knowledge.

KEY CONCEPTS AND FURTHER READING

EXPLANATIONS AND QUESTIONING TECHNIQUES

Lemov, D. (2015) *Teach Like a Champion 2.0: 62 Techniques That Put Students on the Path to College*. New York: John Wiley & Sons.

- This book contains excellent strategies for planning questions that support your explanations.

PLANNING AND SEQUENCING

Rosenshine, B. (2012) Principles of instruction: research-based strategies that all teachers should know. *American Educator*, 36(1): 12–19.

- This article contains excellent guidance on most of the planning principles outlined in this chapter. In particular, it emphasises the need to present ideas one step at a time to build understanding and fluency.

EXPLICIT INSTRUCTION

Willingham, D.T. (2009) *Why Don't Students Like School? A Cognitive Scientist Answers Questions about How the Mind Works and What It Means for the Classroom*. New York: John Wiley & Sons.

- This book provides strong evidence for the benefits of teacher-led instruction and the importance of clear, explicit explanations and ample opportunity to practise.

DUAL CODING

Raichura, P. (2019) *Bunsen Blue*. Available at: www.bunsenblue.wordpress.com

- For examples of different types of dual coding and how they can be used, see the series of blog posts titled 'Clear Teacher Explanations'.

REFERENCES

Ashbee, R. (2018) *Knowledge, Philosophy and Shed Loads of Practice.* Available at: https://rosalindwalker.wordpress.com/2018/06/10/knowledge-philosophy-and-shed-loads-of-practice-my-redrugby-presentation/

Boulton, K. (2017) *My Best Planning: Part 1.* Available at: https://tothereal.wordpress.com/2017/08/12/my-best-planning-part-1/

Christodoulou, D. (2014) *Seven Myths about Education.* London: Routledge.

Clark, J.M. and Paivio, A. (1991) Dual coding theory and education. *Educational Psychology Review*, 3(3): 149–210.

Cowan, N. (2010) The magical mystery four: how is working memory capacity limited, and why? *Current Directions in Psychological Science*, 19(1): 51–7.

Raichura, P. (2018) *Procedural and Declarative Knowledge.* Available at: https://bunsenblue.wordpress.com/2018/05/31/procedural-declarative-knowledge-my-cogscisci-talk/

Reif, F. (2008) *Applying Cognitive Science to Education: Thinking and Learning in Scientific and Other Complex Domains.* Cambridge, MA: MIT Press.

Renkl, A. (2012) Guidance-fading effect. In N.M. Seel (ed.), *Encyclopedia of the Sciences of Learning.* Boston, MA: Springer, pp1400–2.

Rosenshine, B. (2012) Principles of instruction: research-based strategies that all teachers should know. *American Educator*, 36(1): 12–19.

Sumeracki, M.A. and Weinstein, Y. (2018) Optimising learning using retrieval practice. *Impact*, 2: 13–16.

Willingham, D.T. (2009) *Why Don't Students Like School? A Cognitive Scientist Answers Questions about How the Mind Works and What It Means for the Classroom.* New York: John Wiley & Sons.

7

TALK IN THE CLASSROOM

ANDY THARBY

ENGLISH TEACHER AND RESEARCH LEAD, DURRINGTON RESEARCH SCHOOL, WEST SUSSEX, UK

INTRODUCTION

The quality of talk in the classroom has a profound influence on the quality of student learning. This chapter will provide practical advice on both teacher talk and student talk, and will include sections on explaining, questioning and facilitating dialogue and peer-to-peer discussions. The ideas in the chapter relate to section 4 of the Early Career Framework (ECF) on classroom practice.

CHAPTER OBJECTIVES

In this chapter, you will learn:

- to understand how to design and deliver explanations so that your students are able to learn challenging material;
- to understand how to use questioning and dialogue in the classroom so that you can check for understanding and encourage further thinking;
- to understand how to facilitate structured group work and peer-to-peer discussion so that your students can develop their learning and improve their oracy skills.

TEACHER EXPLANATIONS

WHAT IS AN EXPLANATION?

It is impossible to imagine a classroom without teacher explanations. An explanation might take the form of a traditional lecture-style exposition, it might be punctuated by questions, or it might include more visual than verbal input when the subject or topic involves images and symbols. Your explanations will have many purposes: to make something clear and understandable; to expand an idea; to give the reasons, context and consequences of a situation; to show how problems are solved in a step-by-step sequence; or to show the relationships between concepts and facts.

THE ROLE OF PRIOR KNOWLEDGE

It is vital that your explanations are carefully planned in advance. As Willingham (2009) shows, learning happens when students form connections between their prior knowledge and the new material they are covering. Begin your explanation by referring back to the previous task or lesson or by making a connection back to another topic or unit of work. This could take the form of a quiz or a class discussion. Another way to do this is through the use of analogies. For example, a physics teacher might teach the make-up of the hydrogen atom by making an analogy between a mote of dust (the proton) and a tennis court (the empty space in the atom). Analogies like these are more likely to be successful when concrete, familiar and visual items or ideas from everyday life are used to teach abstract and unfamiliar content.

USING EXAMPLES

An effective way to help your students learn challenging concepts and processes is to expose them to multiple examples. Weinstein et al. (2018) highlight that having students work with two or more concrete examples is more effective than having them work with a single concept. A good time to apply this advice comes when teaching new vocabulary. You should explain how the new words apply to two or more contexts and then encourage your students to make connections to even more contexts independently.

Examples are most effective when they are simple, visual, memorable and sensory. They are also effective when they are paired with 'non-examples', which are cases that do not meet the rules for inclusion in the concept itself but shed further light through comparison. For example, a pyramid is a 'non-example' of a triangle, while a frog is a non-example of a mammal. Similarly, you should also consider the difference between 'must-have' elements and 'may-have' elements: a Shakespearean tragedy must end in catastrophe – the death of the tragic hero – but this may be caused by thwarted love; a pentagon must have five sides, but these may be uneven in length.

AVOIDING COGNITIVE OVERLOAD

Cognitive load theory has developed from the work of Australian educational psychologist John Sweller. In the classroom, 'cognitive overload' occurs when the capacity of our students' working memories are exceeded, which often happens if we introduce, or expect them to think about, too many items of complex information in one go.

To reduce the cognitive load of your explanations, you should try the following:

- Break intrinsically difficult material into small parts and teach these one by one, with practice after each step.

- Reduce the amount of redundant and superfluous images and information you present.

- Keep your language concise and precise.

- Repeat key information and points at regular intervals.

- Reduce the length of instructions and provide extra supports and scaffolds when your students have to remember long sequences of information.

- Pair verbal explanations with pictures. This is most effective when these are presented at the same time – known as the contiguity effect.

KEY QUESTIONS

- Think of a topic you have found hard to explain. Why has that been? What strategies could you use to explain it more effectively next time?

- Would the teaching profession become more effective if all teachers were expected to script and rehearse their explanations in advance?

- When is it more effective to deliver learning through an explanation? When is it more effective for students to work collaboratively on their learning?

QUESTIONING

WHY DO TEACHERS ASK QUESTIONS?

If you spend long enough in the classroom of an effective teacher, you are likely to see that questioning and discussion are the cornerstones of their practice and routine. Teachers ask questions for a variety of purposes: to test students' understanding of new content; to encourage and nurture new insights and connections; to ensure that students take a share in the cognitive work of the classroom; to entice students to explore the chief tensions and disputes inherent within the subject discipline; to scaffold the use of subject-specific grammar and vocabulary; and to create a scholarly and collaborative classroom climate.

FEATURES OF EFFECTIVE QUESTIONING

The features of successful questioning (i.e. questioning that enhances students' learning) have been known for some time. Cotton (1988) reviewed a number of studies to show that effective whole-class questioning involves:

- avoiding off-topic questions and focusing on the salient material instead;

- using pacey question sequences for factual, lower-order material;

- leaving a wait time of three seconds or more after posing a more difficult open question;

- redirecting questioning around the room to get as many students involved as possible;

- probing some students' thinking with further questions such as 'Why?' or 'Give me an example to support that';

- praising students sparingly but also avoiding criticism.

Rosenshine's (2012) review of studies into the most effective teaching found that not only did more effective teachers tend to ask more questions than ineffective teachers; they also found ways to check the individual responses of a greater number of students. Interestingly, effective teachers also ask students to explain the processes of their thinking, whereas ineffective teachers are more likely not to do this, instead moving on too swiftly when a student gets a question right or wrong. Finally, Rosenshine (2012) found that good teachers achieved a 'high answer success rate' of about 85 per cent, meaning that the questions were pitched at an optimal level of difficulty – not too hard, but not too easy that they provide no cognitive challenge.

PRACTICAL ADVICE TO IMPROVE QUESTIONING

WHAT SHOULD I DO ABOUT STUDENTS WHO SAY, 'I DON'T KNOW'?

Do not ignore this as there is always a reason. Sometimes a lack of response is caused by a want of effort on the student's part. With a little coaxing and effort, you can help them arrive at an acceptable answer. Another cause might be the question itself, in that it is poorly worded or the student requires extra scaffolding to answer, particularly if it is a very open question. To tackle this, you could try turning it into a closed question by giving two similar options: 'Is the answer x, or is it y?' Once the student has got this correct, you can further challenge them by asking for a justification or another example. A further option is to give the student the correct answer and encourage them to give reasons: 'Okay, the answer to my question is x. How did I come to get this answer?' The third source of 'I don't know' is that your student really does not know! At this point, you will need to decide whether to intervene with the child individually or reteach the whole class.

HOW DO I ENCOURAGE MY STUDENTS TO USE SUBJECT-SPECIFIC GRAMMAR AND VOCABULARY IN THEIR ANSWERS?

Often children will respond to questions in informal grammar and vocabulary. It is important to scaffold their responses so that they begin to speak in an appropriate discourse for the subject. There are two simple strategies that you can use. First, you can ask them to rephrase their answer using the target word: 'Your answer is right, but could you rephrase it using the word "communism" this time?' Second, you can give them a sentence stem to work with: 'I really like the point you were making, but this time can you start with the phrase, "The writer is hinting that ..."?' Ideally, you should aim to pre-empt such situations by giving students sentence stems and vocabulary in advance. In time, you can fade this away and watch them develop the confidence and competence to use the language freely in their verbal responses.

WHAT DO I DO ABOUT THE FACT THAT SOME OF MY STUDENTS DO NOT TAKE PART IN QUESTION-AND-ANSWER SESSIONS?

When students put up their hands, they are indicating that they think they know the answer and are eager to participate. If you only ever pick those students with their hands up, you get a very biased and limited picture of the understanding of your group. Lemov (2015) recommends that teachers should *cold call* instead. This involves asking direct questions irrespective of whether students have their hands up or not. This is advantageous because over time, students learn to expect a question, and as a result are obliged to undertake plenty of silent thinking and rehearsal as they cannot opt out of the discussion.

KEY QUESTIONS

- What types of questions seem to provoke the most thinking from students? Why do you think this is the case?

- How can we support shy and introverted students to become more involved in whole-class questioning?

- How can we provide more opportunities for students to ask their own questions?

COLLABORATIVE TALK AND GROUP WORK

WHY IS COLLABORATIVE TALK IMPORTANT?

Ultimately, the onus for classroom talk should transfer from the teacher to the students, a process involving the gradual handing over of responsibility as students gain increasing independence. This makes logical sense. A class of 30 students engaged in paired discussions will do significantly more thinking than a class of 30 listening to a teacher and a single classmate asking and answering a question. Good-quality talk is so important as it is linked to improved reading skills, improved writing skills and improved learning across the curriculum (EEF, 2019).

Unfortunately, many opportunities for purposeful classroom talk are lost. This is because students need a lot of training, modelling and scaffolding to be successful in collaborative tasks, and often too little time is provided for this.

TIPS FOR FACILITATING STRUCTURED GROUP AND PAIRED DISCUSSIONS

Group and paired tasks are the perfect opportunity to give your students a chance to explore and synthesise their ideas. However, these tasks require careful planning and implementation, especially if your students are not used to working in groups. Too often group work is unsuccessful because the teacher has failed to provide an adequate structure and clear expectations for outcomes.

MODEL AND SCAFFOLD YOUR EXPECTATIONS

Start with your ground rules. What are your expectations in terms of turn-taking, justifying opinions with evidence, and listening to others respectfully? It is a good idea to model these, either with a pre-prepared video or by using a student in the class as your guinea pig. Furthermore, you should aim to provide sentence stems or discussion prompts, especially if the group is new to this kind of work.

PROVIDE A CLEAR GOAL AND TIME CONSTRAINTS

Groups require collective accountability. For example, you might tell your class that in four minutes, they will need to have an answer ready or they will need to present something to the rest of the class. You should usually aim for ambitious time constraints as this will dissuade students from wasting lesson time with off-task behaviour.

GIVE CLEAR ROLES

If you watch a group of students working together for a few minutes, you will notice that work is rarely distributed evenly or fairly. Usually, one or two students will dominate while others will engage in the psychological truism known as 'social loafing'. The assignment of clear roles, such as 'reporter', 'writer' or 'devil's advocate', is very helpful in ensuring that all students know exactly what is required of them.

THINK-PAIR-SHARE

There are few teaching strategies as simple and as effective as this. Ask a question, give students a limited amount of time (usually no more than three to four minutes) to discuss in pairs, and then ask them to feed back to the rest of the group. A golden tip: get into the habit of telling the class that you will randomly choose a pair to share their ideas after the discussion as this again builds accountability.

BUILD SKILLS INCREMENTALLY

If you desire that your students become effective participants in dialogue or group talk, then your best bet is to play the long game. Consider how you will scaffold their talk over weeks, terms and years. What should they be aiming for? How will your long-term plans enable them to get there?

ABANDONMENT IS NOT FAILURE

Sometimes group work is ineffective despite the teacher's best efforts. Ask yourself, 'Do the class really need to work in groups to achieve this learning goal?' There is often a trade-off whereby students work faster and more accurately on independent tasks than they do in groups. Unless you teach a subject that is impossible to participate in without group work (e.g. PE or drama), it is rarely a sign of failure to abandon group work for independent work. Learning should remain your goal; group work is just one way to facilitate learning, and certainly not the only way.

> ## KEY QUESTIONS
>
> - What practical steps could you take to improve collaborative talk in your classroom?
>
> - What are the features of effective and ineffective group work? Why is so much group work in schools so ineffective?
>
> - What role should silence have in a classroom? When might it be more beneficial than talk?

CONCLUSION

This chapter has provided a range of practical strategies for improving talk in the classroom. Ultimately, it has argued that high-quality talk does not happen by magic. Effective teacher talk is almost always the result of careful planning and preparation, especially of explanations and questions. Effective student talk is almost always the result of subtle scaffolding, clear and purposeful task design, and a concerted effort to develop and sustain classroom culture conducive to supportive and collaborative talk.

KEY CONCEPTS AND FURTHER READING

EXPLANATIONS

Centre for Education Statistics and Evaluation (2017) *Cognitive Load Theory: Research That Teachers Really Need to Understand*. Available at: www.cese.nsw.gov.au//images/stories/PDF/cognitive-load-theory-VR_AA3.pdf

- This provides a helpful overview of cognitive load theory and may be helpful for planning explanations that avoid cognitive overload.

Tharby, A. (2018) *How to Explain Absolutely Anything to Absolutely Anyone: The Art and Science of Teacher Explanation*. Carmarthen: Crown House.

- This book sets out an evidence-informed approach to help teachers explain complex concepts in a way that students will understand and remember.

QUESTIONING

Allison, S. and Tharby, A. (2015) *Making Every Lesson Count: Six Principles to Support Great Teaching and Learning*. Carmarthen: Crown House.

- This book offers practical strategies to support effective teaching and includes case studies of excellent practice – Chapter 6 is on questioning.

Cotton, K. (1988) *Close-Up #5: Classroom Questioning*. Available at: http://educationnorthwest.org/sites/default/files/ClassroomQuestioning.pdf

- This summary discusses research on classroom questioning and offers recommendations based on the findings.

COLLABORATIVE TALK AND GROUP WORK

Education Endowment Foundation (EEF) (2019) *Improving Literacy in Secondary Schools*. Available at: https://educationendowmentfoundation.org.uk/tools/guidance-reports/improving-literacy-in-secondary-schools/

- This guidance report includes advice on providing opportunities for structured talk.

REFERENCES

Cotton, K. (1988) *Close-Up #5: Classroom Questioning*. Available at: http://educationnorthwest.org/sites/default/files/ClassroomQuestioning.pdf

Education Endowment Foundation (EEF) (2019) *Improving Literacy in Secondary Schools*. Available at: https://educationendowmentfoundation.org.uk/tools/guidance-reports/improving-literacy-in-secondary-schools/

Lemov, D. (2015) *Teach Like a Champion 2.0: 62 Techniques That Put Students on the Path to College*. San Francisco, CA: Jossey-Bass.

Rosenshine, B. (2012) Principles of instruction: research-based strategies that all teachers should know. *American Educator*, 36(1): 12–19.

Weinstein, Y., Madan, C.R. and Sumeracki, M.A. (2018) Teaching the science of learning. *Cognitive Research: Principles and Implications*, 3(2): 1–17.

Willingham, D. (2009) *Why Don't Students Like School? A Cognitive Scientist Answers Questions about How the Mind Works and What It Means for the Classroom*. San Francisco, CA: Jossey-Bass.

8

ADAPTING TEACHING

CHRISTIAN BOKHOVE

ASSOCIATE PROFESSOR IN MATHEMATICS EDUCATION, UNIVERSITY OF SOUTHAMPTON, UK

RYAN CAMPBELL

VICE PRINCIPAL, HIGH SCHOOL CURRICULUM AND LEARNING, JAKARTA INTERNATIONAL SCHOOL, INDONESIA

INTRODUCTION

This chapter covers a lot of ground, but at its core is the idea that expert adaptive teaching can be seen as a 'guidance dilemma': when to give what amount of guidance to optimise learning. The chapter directly addresses several sections of the Early Career Framework (ECF), such as in promoting good progress (section 2), planning and teaching well-structured lessons (section 4), and adaptive teaching (section 5). Given this extensive range of sections, it would be best to see the content of this chapter as a starting point for these topics, not a complete overview; further reading is given at the end of the chapter.

> ## CHAPTER OBJECTIVES
>
> After reading this chapter, you will:
>
> - understand more about the role of prior knowledge in learning, spaced practice, expertise reversal, and the voyage from being a novice towards becoming more expert;
>
> - understand how scaffolding can support students, and how such scaffolding can be done through guidance, feedback and teaching strategies;
>
> - receive suggestions on how using resources effectively can support learning (e.g. peer support, the use of textbooks).

THE ROLE OF PRIOR KNOWLEDGE

One of the most important variables to get right in the classroom is a teacher's judgement of what level of prior knowledge students have. On the one hand, this can be gauged by good lesson planning and a solid scheme of work in your department. On the other hand, it requires the adaptive skill set to judge student understanding and respond accordingly. This does not always have to be in a test or quiz form as one-to-one support, questioning and whole-class discussions can all usefully inform your professional judgement. We could see this critical issue as a case of determining the level of expertise your students have on any given topic and then activating that prior knowledge. This, in turn, will determine the amount and type of support you will give as a teacher. Just this short introduction has already introduced several crucial aspects: first, ensure that prior knowledge is gauged and activated – spacing, retrieval and interleaving can help here; second, what these levels mean for a student's location on his or her journal from novice to expert; and finally, how differing levels of prior knowledge mean that choosing the 'best' approach is not always as clear-cut as it seems.

SPACING, RETRIEVAL AND INTERLEAVED PRACTICE

One of the oldest and most robust effects in education, the spacing effect, is the simple but powerful idea that repeated exposures to material strengthens learning. Spaced practice and its close cousin interleaving have been studied and shown to be effective strategies across a wide variety of settings, from language learning to physical education (Bjork and Bjork, 2019). Spaced practice can often be combined with retrieval practice, the idea that going through the effort of recalling previously learnt material to mind strengthens learning. Retrieval practice has a robust evidence base, regardless of the method used with evidence of a retrieval practice effect from quizzing, short answers and use of concept maps. As well as providing variety to your lesson planning, the key point here is that it is the act of effortful retrieval that deepens learning rather than the method itself. It is important, though, that retrieval practice incorporates a range of both fact-based and more higher-order questions or prompts, even with beginner learners (Agarwal, 2019). The spacing effect does require some scheduling on the part of the teacher to ensure that course content is covered equally in subsequent lessons after initial teaching. Interleaving, or mixing practice of more than one topic within a subject domain, appears to be a particularly efficient way to organise practice, with strong evidence for the effectiveness of interleaving – if allied with corrective feedback – in the mathematics classroom (Rohrer et al., 2019).

FROM NOVICE TO EXPERT

With students retrieving and rehearsing prior knowledge, even after one lesson students' prior knowledge will have changed. Some students will be less of a novice than they were in the beginning as they will have become more expert. Such levels of expertise therefore play an important part in the learning of students. When does a student cease to be a novice, and when can we start to call them experts? This very much depends on the definition of an expert. For example, if we look at the research by Anders Ericsson, an expert is someone who has achieved true mastery of their subject and has probably spent at least ten years engaged in so-called deliberate practice (Ericsson and Pool, 2016). Some of the features of such practice are:

- it's designed specifically to improve performance;

- it can be repeated a lot;

- feedback on results is continuously available;

- it's highly demanding mentally;

- it isn't much fun.

However, the presence of those features does not necessarily mean that it is deliberate practice. Deliberate practice leads to fuller mental representations of both knowledge and skills. Another researcher who looked at experts in her research is Michelene Chi (see Chi et al., 1982). She observed that knowledge structures are more cohesive and integrated in experts, and that they can use their knowledge structure in ways that novices cannot, such as helping them learn and assimilate new concepts and make decisions about familiar concepts. Another term for such mental representations and knowledge structures is 'schemas'. We could therefore reformulate our challenge of gauging prior knowledge as what the already present schemas of students are and how they are influenced by even just teaching a lesson. Stellan Ohlsson (2011) describes how there might be five distinct types of information that might be 'available at the outset of practice: direct instructions; declarative knowledge about the task; strategies for analogous tasks; demonstrations, models and solved examples; and outcomes of unselective search' (p194).

EXPERTISE REVERSAL

One approach is to just teach the content well, regardless of students' prior knowledge. The catch is that even after one lesson on a topic, the information might not be novel any more. In addition, some subjects, such as languages and mathematics, are hierarchical: novel information *builds* on prior information. But what is the worst that could happen if a student is already relatively expert? Research into so-called aptitude–treatment interaction (ATI) demonstrates that differences in aptitude and traits can mean different effects for different instructional methods (Cronbach and Snow, 1977). More recently, ATI has also underpinned an 'expertise reversal effect' (Kalyuga et al., 2003), which emphasises the importance of providing novices with guidance, and in turn gradually removing guidance as expertise and knowledge in long-term memory (i.e. mental representations, schemas) grows. If guidance is not gradually reduced, then instructional methods suitable for beginners can backfire and even decrease learning for relative experts.

IMPLICATIONS

What can we take from all of this? If we agree that prior knowledge determines appropriate teaching strategies and we can also agree that learners might be more or less relatively expert from the outset or even after a short teaching session, there is a place for a nuanced approach to teaching strategies. As Kalyuga and Singh (2016) point out, educational debates are often presented as a dichotomy between extreme positions when the messy reality of classroom practice is more mixed. Your view on guidance and learning can incorporate a wider variety of definitions of guidance adapted to the learning goals of the activity and learner expertise. We will now consider how scaffolding and guidance can help with this.

SCAFFOLDING AND FADING

Just like Rome wasn't built in one day, this can best be done gradually, first with more support (scaffolding), and then gradually less support will be needed (fading).

SCAFFOLDING

Mainly associated with Jerome Bruner, whose theory of scaffolding emerged as part of social constructivist theory, scaffolding means any action to bridge the gap in knowledge between existing and new knowledge by a teacher or more knowledgeable peer. Bruner described the constant interaction between a teacher and a student as scaffolding: 'scaffolding consists essentially of the adult "controlling" those elements of the task that are initially beyond the learner's capacity, thus permitting him to concentrate upon and complete only those elements that are within his range of competence' (Wood et al., 1976, p90).

Bruner believed that when children start to learn new concepts, they need help from teachers and other adults in the form of active support. First, learners are dependent on adult support, but as they become more independent in their thinking and acquire new skills and knowledge, the support can be gradually faded away. One particular way of 'removing scaffolding' is in the way that practice becomes less and less concrete, something especially effective with younger children. Fyfe and colleagues describe this 'Bruner-inspired' phenomenon as 'concreteness fading'. This is an approach that begins with concrete materials and gradually fades towards more abstract ones. This concreteness fading technique 'exploits the continuum from concreteness to abstractness and allows learners to initially benefit from the grounded, concrete context while still encouraging them to generalize beyond it' (Fyfe et al., 2014, p10).

FADING FEEDBACK

Another way to remove scaffolding is to decrease the amount of feedback a teacher gives. There are numerous studies which have shown that fading guidance contributes to better learning outcomes (e.g. Atkinson et al., 2003). For example, in the context of providing information through fully worked examples, a number of studies have shown that after worked solution steps were gradually removed, learners had to determine the missing steps on their own. Other studies show that fading prompts and feedback work better than continuous prompting. And as learners eventually have to 'stand on their own two feet' and become independent learners, it makes more sense to remove support gradually. The advantage of guidance begins to decrease only when learners have sufficient prior knowledge to provide 'internal' guidance. The speed of fading can even be dependent on an individual's progress by providing less feedback when a prior learning milestone has been reached. It is for this reason that 'personalisation' can also be seen as an opportunity to take into account prior knowledge.

GUIDANCE DILEMMA

How should learning environments balance information or giving and withholding guidance to achieve optimal student learning? How best to achieve this balance remains a challenging problem in instructional science.

We can call this problem the 'guidance dilemma' or 'assistance dilemma'. One context in which this has been studied quite frequently is in technology support, and just like with the feedback research by Hattie and Timperley (2007), it turns out that there are many variables at play when deciding this, such as the timing and spacing of the feedback support (e.g. immediate, delayed), the detail level of the feedback guidance, the focus of the feedback (e.g. task, process, self-regulation, self), or the presentation of the feedback. The organisation of the guidance also determines the level of challenge for a learner. The assistance dilemma can be seen as being related to Bjork's 'desirable difficulties' and the notion that while assisting performance during instruction can sometimes improve learning, in some cases making performance more difficult during instruction improves learning (Schmidt and Bjork, 1992). Whatever choice you make as a teacher, we would argue that rather than always relying on one strategy, you look at the context, your students, prior knowledge and the resources available, and choose your teaching strategies accordingly.

KEY QUESTIONS

- Under which circumstances might more real-world 'authentic' tasks help or hinder student learning?

- What are three ways you could scaffold learning in your subject area?

- How are you making sure you hit the 'Goldilocks spot' – not too difficult but not too easy? How will you do this for a whole class full of students?

USING RESOURCES EFFECTIVELY

At the end of the previous section, we acknowledged one variable that determines what a realistic teaching strategy is: the resources that are available. We therefore finish this chapter with some words on effective use of resources. We take a broad view of resources to include textbooks and teaching materials, but also 'knowledgeable others', including students' peers.

PEER FEEDBACK

Peer feedback, using peers to give learning feedback on the work of other students, does appear to have a wealth of evidence to support its use in the classroom, with potential learning benefits for both the peer being assessed and the peer doing the assessing (Double et al., 2019). Applicable to any peer-to-peer written comments, grading, or verbal feedback, peer feedback can take a wide variety of forms, and the most effective to include in your professional toolbox are as follows:

- *Scaffolding/marking rubrics*. Despite some general criticisms of rubrics, in the context of peer assessment they do provide guidance for peer markers and limit peer markers overscoring their peers.

- *Teacher modelling*. An important way of ensuring that peer feedback is used to enhance learning is for the teacher to model how to interpret rubrics and what is high-quality feedback.

- *Online.* Online peer feedback is a potent way of streamlining the process of peer feedback and has been shown to be an effective way of using peer assessment.

- *Anonymity.* There are mixed views in the literature on whether or not peer feedback should be anonymous. With the evidence mixed, it is probably worth experimenting in your own practice to find which way or which combination of ways work for you as a developing professional.

GROUP WORK

Group work is a topic that can often generate more heat than light, with strong arguments put forward by both proposers and opposers. The evidence from the relevant literature suggests that both are correct, and that group work can have limitations and strengths. Overall, group work can be a very useful tool if certain cognitive and social boundary conditions are met (Campbell and Bokhove, 2019). Beginning with the social limitations, group work is often dismissed with phrases such as 'free-rider' and 'social loafing', describing the tendency of some group members to contribute less than they would individually and instead rely on the efforts of the rest of the group. Similarly, status issues can arise, and group members can defer to higher-status people's ideas regardless of their merit, as well as seek to subtly undermine the best performers, who also can be guilty of lowering their own performance to fit in with the rest of the group. However, taking into account these caveats, there are also some areas where group work can provide benefits, such as reducing cognitive load by pooling working memory resources across the group, improving motivation, in-built error correction, and discussing different perspectives, which can lead to deeper learning.

So, how best to benefit from the strengths of group work while avoiding some of the limitations? First of all, both a shared goal and individual accountability are necessary (but not sufficient) preconditions to achieve successful group work (Slavin, 2010). Furthermore, the nature of the goal is crucial, and the principles of goal-setting theory apply – you should work to ensure that your students are committed to the group goal, perhaps by involving them in its formation, or at least explaining the reason for the goal. Learning goals (e.g. 'Discover four or five different ways of doing *x* or *y*') rather than outcome goals (e.g. 'Achieve an A grade') are better for beginner learners. Lastly, it is almost certainly a good idea to establish and monitor the use of group norms.

DO NOT REINVENT THE WHEEL: EFFECTIVELY USE RESOURCES

As we discussed in the previous sections, students can be valuable learning resources for each other as long as you plan purposefully. Some of the evidence-based strategies you may wish to try are combining conceptual MCQs with peer discussion of appropriate answers, students teaching other students, and elaborative interrogation. Another useful way to support your teaching can lie in the use of textbooks. As Oates (2014) noted, 'High quality textbooks support both teachers and pupils – they free teachers up to concentrate on refining pedagogy and developing engaging, effective learning' (p4). This is an important nuance as textbooks can provide clear delineation of content and a coherent learning progression within the subject when allied with teacher expertise. Furthermore, textbooks can represent curriculum content, and can therefore be seen as an 'intended curriculum', hopefully with 'curriculum coherence'. Well-constructed textbooks not only support teachers, but also provide support for pupils to work independently out of class. For this reason, it is advisable to not just blindly choose a textbook, but to critically evaluate before you use them, including suitable older textbooks.

As an example, textbooks from the School Mathematics Project (SMP) were deemed more mathematically coherent than a rival textbook (Hodgen et al., 2010), and textbook series from the 1960s and onwards remain worthwhile resources for teachers today.

> ## KEY QUESTIONS
>
> - Are there resources such as textbooks and worksheets that can help you support your lessons?
>
> - In what way do these resources fit in the 'grander scheme' (i.e. how do they fit in the curriculum)?
>
> - How can you make sure that peer feedback and group work enhance learning?

CONCLUSION

Many of the aspects described in this chapter have been tabulated by other researchers. Some will, for example, note similarities with popular work by Rosenshine (2010), ranging from instructional elements but also the gradual release of guidance towards independent practice. Rather than a 'whole system', it should best be seen as a set of principles derived from various sources, within which decisions ultimately have to be left to a teacher's professional judgement. This combination of evidence-informed principles and craft knowledge, in which contextual factors from schools and classrooms are taken into account, forms the most effective education. If we start to frame students' learning, notwithstanding other educational aims and outcomes, as a voyage from novice to 'more expert', we can say that the best teaching approaches are not one size fits all, but instead are flexible approaches incorporating and adapting to the prior knowledge and guidance needed to become more expert.

KEY CONCEPTS AND FURTHER READING

SPACING, RETRIEVAL AND INTERLEAVING

You can get a good idea about all three concepts in Rohrer et al. (2009).

EXPERTISE

You can read more about expertise in the work of Ericsson and Pool (2016) or Part 3 of Ohlsson (2011). With some instructional strategies, expertise reversal can take place. Kalyuga et al. (2003) is the seminal source.

SCAFFOLDING

The review article on 'concreteness fading' by Fyfe et al. (2014) is a good starting point. If you can get a hold of the Bruner references in that article, it is always informative to read what the 'classics' said.

FADING

Gradually reducing guidance, so-called fading, can be looked at in detail. Atkinson et al. (2003) is the seminal article on fading worked-out steps. The general role of feedback is covered well in Hattie and Timperley (2007).

RESOURCE USE

Teacher resources come in many forms. More on working with peers is in Double et al. (2019). Several relevant references regarding group work are in Campbell and Bokhove (2019).

━━━━━ REFERENCES ━━━━━

Agarwal, P.K. (2019) Retrieval practice and Bloom's taxonomy: do students need fact knowledge before higher-order learning? *Journal of Educational Psychology*, 111(2): 189–209.

Atkinson, R.K., Renkl, A. and Merrill, M. (2003) Transitioning from studying examples to solving problems: effects of self-explanation prompts and fading worked-out steps. *Journal of Educational Psychology*, 95(4): 774–83.

Bjork, R.A. and Bjork, E.L. (2019) The myth that blocking one's study or practice by topic or skill enhances learning. In C. Barton (ed.), *Education Myths: An Evidence-Informed Guide for Teachers*. Woodbridge: John Catt Educational, pp57–70.

Campbell, R. and Bokhove, C. (2019) Building learning culture through effective uses of group work. *Impact*, 5: 12–15.

Chi, M.T.H., Glaser, R. and Rees, E. (1982) Expertise in problem solving. In R. Sternberg (ed.), *Advances in the Psychology of Human Intelligence*. Hillsdale, NJ: Erlbaum, pp7–75.

Cronbach, L.J. and Snow, R.E. (1977) *Aptitudes and Instructional Methods: A Handbook for Research on Interactions*. New York: Irvington.

Double, K.S., McGrane, J.A. and Hopfenbeck, T.N. (2019) The impact of peer assessment on academic performance: a meta-analysis of control group studies. *Educational Psychological Review*. doi:10.1007/s10648-019-09510-3

Ericsson, A. and Pool, R. (2016) *Peak: Secrets from the New Science of Expertise*. Boston, MA: Houghton Mifflin Harcourt.

Fyfe, E., McNeil, N., Son, J. and Goldstone, R. (2014) Concreteness fading in mathematics and science instruction: a systematic review. *Educational Psychology Review*, 26(1): 9–25.

Hattie, J. and Timperley, H. (2007) The power of feedback. *Review of Educational Research*, 77(1): 81–112.

Hodgen, J., Kuchemann, D. and Brown, M. (2010) Textbooks for the teaching of algebra in lower secondary school: are they informed by research? *Pedagogies: An International Journal*, 5(3): 187–201.

Kalyuga, S. and Singh, A. (2016) Rethinking the boundaries of cognitive load theory in complex learning. *Educational Psychological Review*, 28(4): 831–52.

Kalyuga, S., Ayres, P., Chandler, P. and Sweller, J. (2003) The expertise reversal effect. *Educational Psychologist*, 38(1): 23–31.

Oates, T. (2014) *Why Textbooks Count*. Cambridge: Cambridge Assessment.

Ohlsson, S. (2011) *Deep Learning: How the Mind Overrides Experience*. Cambridge: Cambridge University Press.

Rohrer, D., Dedrick, R.F., Hartwig, M.K. and Cheung, C.-N. (2019) A randomized controlled trial of interleaved mathematics practice. *Journal of Educational Psychology*, 112(1): 40–52.

Rosenshine, B. (2010) *Principles of Instruction*. Available at: www.ibe.unesco.org/fileadmin/user_upload/Publications/Educational_Practices/EdPractices_21.pdf

Schmidt, R.A. and Bjork, R.A. (1992) New conceptualizations of practice: common principles in three paradigms suggest new concepts for training. *Psychological Science*, 3(4): 207–18.

Slavin, R.E. (2010) Co-operative learning: what makes group-work work? In H. Dumont, D. Istance and F. Benavides (eds), *The Nature of Learning: Using Research to Inspire Practice*. Paris: OECD, pp161–78.

Wood, D., Bruner, J.S. and Ross, G. (1976) The role of tutoring in problem solving. *Journal of Child Psychology and Psychiatry*, 17(2): 89–100.

9

SUPPORTING STUDENTS WITH SPECIAL EDUCATIONAL NEEDS AND DISABILITIES

SIMON KNIGHT

CO-HEAD OF FRANK WISE SCHOOL, OXFORDSHIRE, UK

KAREN WESPIESER

DIRECTOR OF OPERATIONS, DRIVER YOUTH TRUST, LONDON, UK

INTRODUCTION

When you enter the classroom for the first time, it is important to remember that you are embarking on the very beginning of a long-term professional journey. Gaining qualified teacher status (QTS) means that you are broadly at a point where you are able to be responsible for the education of the children you teach, but you are far from being an expert. This is particularly the case when looking to support children who present with complexity in the classroom, including those who are identified as having a special educational need or disability (SEND).

According to the Children and Families Act 2014 (Section 20), a child has special educational needs 'if he or she has a learning difficulty or disability which calls for special educational provision to be made for him or her'. Special educational provision is 'educational or training provision that is additional to, or different from, that made generally for others of the same age in mainstream schools in England'.

A child of compulsory school age (5–16 years) has a learning difficulty or disability if he or she has:

> (a) significantly greater difficulty in learning than the majority of others of the same age, or (b) has a disability which prevents him or her from making use of facilities of a kind generally provided for others of the same age in mainstream schools.

> (DfE and DoH, 2015, para xiv)

These are facts that you probably already know following your training. But what might this look like in practice in your classroom? This chapter will look at the barriers to learning, the SEND code of practice and the graduated approach, and working with colleagues to support learning.

It is likely that you will have had a different experience during initial teacher education (ITE) to some of your colleagues, and as such may well have differing levels of experience with regard to the education of children with SEND. While this may feel disconcerting, particularly if you have had limited experience, it is important to recognise that this will be the case for many early career teachers as a result of the variety of SEND content and practice provided through different ITE courses, routes and placements.

Expertise takes time to shape, and there should be no shame in acknowledging the things that you do least well and seeking support to enable you to do them more effectively over time. In his pop art classic *Drowning Girl*, Roy Lichtenstein depicts a woman sinking below the waves uttering the words, 'I don't care! I'd rather sink than call Brad for help!' It is really important that as an early career teacher, you don't find yourself in a similar position. Fortunately, the SEND community is a generous one and one that is very willing to offer support. So, treat your emerging understanding of SEND as a key part of your professional journey and see your honesty about what you need to improve as a professional strength. In doing so, you will begin to be able to raise your complexity threshold, and over time the things that confound you now will begin to become second nature.

BARRIERS TO LEARNING

Needs of students are split into four broad areas – communication and interaction, cognition and learning, social, emotional and mental health difficulties, and sensory and/or physical needs – and 11 primary areas of need (see Table 9.1). However, students often also have significant difficulties in more than one area (Rutter et al., 1970), and in some cases difficulties in one area will cause difficulties in another. Having said that, having an idea of the prevalence of different types of need may help you prioritise and consider where you might like to increase your knowledge.

Table 9.1   The four areas of need

Communication and interaction	Cognition and learning	Social, emotional and mental health difficulties	Sensory and/or physical needs
• Speech, language and communication needs (SLCN) • Autistic spectrum disorder (ASD)	• Specific learning difficulty (SpLD) • Moderate learning difficulty (MLD) • Profound and multiple learning difficulty (PMLD) • Severe learning difficulty (SLD)	• Social, emotional and mental health (SEMH)	• Hearing impairment (HI) • Physical disability (PD) • Multisensory impairment (MSI) • Visual impairment (VI)

The first thing to realise, however, is that this will depend significantly on what phase of education you teach. Special schools count for just two in every ten students with a special educational need. Eight in ten are in mainstream schools, but the profile of SEND in primary and secondary schools (and potentially the support that you get) is very different.

Overall, around 15 per cent of the school population has a SEND, but this figure is slightly higher in primary schools than in secondary schools. The type of need is also different. For example, in primary school, speech, language and communication needs (SLCN) is the most common area of need (accounting for more than half of all cases of SEND in reception-age children), but by Year 11 SLCN is relatively rare, with just one in ten of all SEND students having this as their primary area of need. Conversely, specific learning difficulty (SpLD) is rarely identified in very young learners, but accounts for a quarter of all SEND by the end of schooling.

Understanding that SEND is not a fixed attribute, either of students or of the school system, is vital. Identifying the broad area of need is a useful first step, but a more detailed understanding of need is required for action. To support students with SEND, you will need to not only decide whether a student has a SEND; you should also identify the individual characteristics of their needs.

THE SEND CODE OF PRACTICE

The SEND code of practice is the official guidance document relating to SEND. It focuses on a family-centred system of care and education that spans the four broad areas of special educational needs and support.

The key mantra that teachers need to take from the code of practice is, 'Every teacher is a teacher of SEND'. Classroom teachers have responsibility for the progress of all students within their class, including those with SEND, and the code of practice recommends that this happens within a framework known as the graduated approach.

The graduated approach has four stages of action: assess, plan, do and review.

ASSESS

In identifying a child as needing SEND support, the teacher, working with the special educational needs coordinator (SENCO) and the student's parents, carries out an analysis of the student's needs. This initial assessment should be reviewed regularly to ensure that support is matched to need. Where there is little or no improvement in the student's progress, more specialist assessment may be called for from specialist teachers or from health and social services or other agencies beyond the setting. Where professionals are not already working with the setting, the SENCO will contact them, with the parents' agreement.

PLAN

Where it is decided to provide SEND support, and having formally notified the parents, the teacher and the SENCO agree, in consultation with the parents, the outcomes they are seeking, the interventions and support to be put in place, the expected impact on progress, development or behaviour, and a clear date for review. Plans should take into account the views of the student. The support and intervention provided should be selected to meet the outcomes identified for the student, based on reliable evidence of effectiveness, and provided by practitioners with relevant skills and knowledge. Parents should be involved in planning support and, where appropriate, in reinforcing the provision or contributing to progress at home.

DO

The teacher remains responsible for working with the student on a daily basis. With support from the SENCO, they should oversee the implementation of the interventions or programmes agreed as part of SEND support. The SENCO will support you in assessing the child's response to the action taken, in problem-solving, and in advising on the effective implementation of support.

REVIEW

The effectiveness of the support and its impact on the child's progress should be reviewed in line with the agreed date. The impact and quality of the support should be evaluated by the practitioner and the SENCO, working with the student's parents and taking into account the student's views. They should agree any changes to the outcomes and support for the child in light of the child's progress and development. Parents should have clear information about the impact of the support provided and be involved in planning next steps.

This cycle of action is then revisited in increasing detail and with increasing frequency to identify the best way of securing good progress.

WORKING WITH COLLEAGUES TO SUPPORT LEARNING

They say it takes a village to raise a child, and that is never truer than when supporting students with SEND. As exemplified in the code of practice, when you are working within the graduated approach, you will be working alongside a range of other adults, including parents, SENCOs and specialist professionals.

SENCOs

The adult in your school who is likely to have the most experience and expertise when it comes to students with SEND is your SENCO. A SENCO is responsible for the day-to-day operation of the school's SEND policy. All mainstream schools must appoint a teacher to be their SENCO. While you must take the lead – indeed the responsibility – for students with SEND in your class, the SENCO is a fount of knowledge that you can and should draw on.

Regular professional discussions with your SENCO about students in your class with SEND are essential. You will want to discuss with them the barriers to learning, where progress is being made (and importantly where it isn't), interventions that are being put in place and the impact these are having – not just on learning, but on the wellbeing of the student – and any impact on the rest of the class.

Your SENCO can also be your gateway to further training, reading or evidence that you might seek to further support students with SEND in your class, this year and in years to come.

PARENTS

A good starting point for developing a better understanding of complex children is building strong relationships with families. The expertise developed through lived experience is quite possibly the greatest source of untapped expertise available to teachers. While it may initially seem slightly unusual to ask the families of the children you teach to help you do so successfully, doing so is an investment worth making and a sign of professional maturity.

In the SEND Reflection Framework (Whole School SEND, 2017), a free-to-access online document to support critical reflection around SEND classroom practice, the section on working with families states quite clearly that:

> *An effective partnership with the student's family is essential in building and maintaining a trusting relationship and in supporting successful family participation. Developing your ability to communicate successfully with families can help to build positive relationships and can support the gathering of supplementary information to maximise the impact of school on the student and their broader educational development.*
>
> (p23)

It goes on to offer a range of different affirmative statements that, as an early career teacher, there would be value in exploring with colleagues in order to strengthen your ability to develop effective relationships with families. This should be done through thoughtful discussion, in the knowledge that there are not necessarily specific right and wrong answers, but rather approaches that are more or less likely to work effectively.

There is also value in taking the time to read the leaflet *A Guide to Making Conversations Count for All Families* (Whole School SEND, 2018). This document, written by families as part of the Ask Listen Do project hosted by the NHS, takes the principles of the SEND Reflection Framework but presents them as questions for families to ask schools. This can act as a useful checklist of the sort of things you should be developing an understanding of, and as such provide answers to, should you be asked.

TEACHING ASSISTANTS

Another area in which to invest time at the start of your career is the effective deployment of teaching assistants (TAs). The highly significant and impactful work of Peter Blatchford, Rob Webster and others, and its evolution into the Maximising the Impact of Teaching Assistants project, sets out a compelling evidence base for getting the most out of the other adults in your classroom. The documentation published by the Education Endowment Foundation (EEF, 2018) highlights seven recommendations, presented as an easily accessible poster. The key messages are:

1.   TAs should not be used as an informal teaching resource for low-attaining students.

2.   Use TAs to add value to what teachers do, not replace them.

3.   Use TAs to help students develop independent learning skills and manage their own learning.

4.   Ensure TAs are fully prepared for their role in the classroom.

5.   Provide high-quality one-to-one and small group support using structured interventions.

6.   Adopt evidence-based interventions to support TAs in their small group and one-to-one instruction.

7.   Ensure explicit connections are made between learning from everyday classroom teaching structured interventions.

Considering carefully the implications of both the effective and ineffective use of TAs on the learning behaviours and outcomes of the students can help to ensure that all students get the very best education possible.

SPECIAL SCHOOLS AND ALTERNATIVE PROVISION

There is also much to be gained by strengthening relationships with your local special schools, alternative provision and student referral units. One of the challenges the education sector faces is that while there is significant SEND expertise within the system, it is not always in the right volume or the right locations necessary to impact positively on children in classrooms. It is important to recognise that the specialist sector is not the gatekeeper of some form of alternative pedagogy, but rather the implementer of pedagogy in different ways – ways that can often be applied successfully in the mainstream classroom.

A starting point for any early career teacher is taking the time to arrange to visit the specialist providers local to them. Many will offer classroom access through open mornings or similar professional learning opportunities. However, visits in isolation are unlikely to transform what you do in your own classroom. When investing in developing your knowledge and understanding of classroom complexity, consider the evidence set out within the *Standard for Teachers' Professional Development* (DfE, 2016). This document makes use of the comprehensive evidence base around high-impact professional development and references a wide range of research and further reading to support your emerging understanding of what effective professional development looks like.

When visiting schools that specialise in teaching children and young people with SEND, some of the things that you may wish to explore are as follows:

- *Assessment methodologies and tools.* Learning how to better understand the variety of ways in which developmental delays or atypical developmental pathways can be identified is likely to enable better targeted teaching. If we do not have a clear understanding of why a child's learning is going in a direction different to that expected, then we may not be focusing on supporting the areas that will have the greatest impact.

- *How learning is broken down.* Seeking support on how to successfully deconstruct learning objectives, in order to establish which specific concept is causing the developmental difficulty, is a key area to invest in. The specialist sector is often a good source of knowledge when it comes to forensically investigating the various interrelationships between concepts and how they can impact on learning outcomes.

- *Curriculum structures.* Curriculum, as well as its design and implementation, has become a significant focus in recent times, ostensibly as a result of the changes that Ofsted made to the education inspection framework (EIF) (Ofsted, 2019). Part of the focus has been on the effective sequencing of learning. Investing time in understanding how special schools in particular do this, as a result of their long-standing commitment to interpreting curricula in the best interests of the children they teach, is likely to be time well spent.

- *Effective communication.* The specialist sector uses a wide range of different approaches to ensure that communication is well matched to the developmental level of the children they teach. This includes using assessment tools such as the Derbyshire Language Scheme (Knowles and Masidlover, 1982) to determine levels of comprehension and expression, symbol-based communication, or signing approaches such as Makaton. Further developing your understanding of how to support effective communication can have a broad-ranging impact on how you can enable children to further develop their communicative confidence and capability.

To help you develop your professional learning further, a significant source of information, resources and training opportunities associated with SEND can be found on the SEND Gateway (**www.sendgateway.org.uk**). Seeing the development of your knowledge and understanding of children with SEND as being integral to your continuing professional learning, as well as spending time exploring the various documents and opportunities available, will support you in embarking on a journey of professional curiosity that will ultimately benefit all of the children that you teach.

KEY QUESTIONS

- What are the most common primary areas of need experienced by students in your school? How might you support these students using the graduated approach?

- What key information do you need from your SENCO and what key information do you have to communicate? How can you ensure that information flows between yourself and the SENCO, and who else might you need to consult with?

- How can you engage the families of students with SEND? Is there such a thing as too much engagement? How will you work with hard-to-reach families?

After all, effective teaching for children with SEND is really just very good teaching, and becoming a very good teacher is something we should all be aspiring to.

KEY CONCEPTS AND FURTHER READING

- SEND is a broad term that contains a multitude of different areas of need:

Webster, R. and Blatchford, P. (2019) Making sense of 'teaching', 'support' and 'differentiation': the educational experiences of students with education, health and care plans and statements in mainstream secondary schools. *European Journal of Special Needs Education*, 34(1): 98–113.

- SEND is not a fixed attribute, either of students or of the school system:

Johnson, H. and Bradley, L. (2017) *SEN Support: A Survey of Schools and Colleges*. London: DfE.

- Every teacher is a teacher of SEND, but teaching students with SEND doesn't happen in isolation – it's a team effort:

Skipp, A. and Hopwood, V. (2017) *SEN Support: Case Studies from Schools and College*. London: DfE.

REFERENCES

Department for Education (DfE) (2016) *Standard for Teachers' Professional Development*. Available at: https://assets.publishing.service.gov.uk/government/uploads/system/uploads/attachment_data/file/537031/160712_-_PD_Expert_Group_Guidance.pdf

Department for Education (DfE) and Department of Health (DoH) (2015) *SEN Code of Practice: 0 to 25 Years*. Available at: www.gov.uk/government/publications/send-code-of-practice-0-to-25

Education Endowment Foundation (EEF) (2018) *Making the Best Use of Teaching Assistants*. Available at: https://educationendowmentfoundation.org.uk/public/files/Publications/Teaching_Assistants/TA_Recommendations Summary.pdf

HM Government (2014) *Children and Families Act 2014*. Available at: www.legislation.gov.uk/ukpga/2014/6/contents/enacted

Knowles, W. and Masidlover, M. (1982) *The Derbyshire Language Scheme*. Derbyshire: Derbyshire County Council.

Ofsted (2019) *Education Inspection Framework*. Available at: https://assets.publishing.service.gov.uk/government/uploads/system/uploads/attachment_data/file/801429/Education_inspection_framework.pdf

Rutter, M., Tizard, J. and Whitmore, K. (1970) *Education, Health and Behaviour*. London: Longmans.

Whole School SEND (2017) *SEND Reflection Framework*. Available at: www.sendgateway.org.uk/r/sendreflection-framework.html

Whole School SEND (2018) *A Guide to Making Conversations Count for All Families*. Available at: www.sendgateway.org.uk/r/makingconversationswithschools.html

10

DEVELOPING LITERACY IN SECONDARY SCHOOLS

ALEX QUIGLEY

NATIONAL CONTENT MANAGER, EDUCATION ENDOWMENT FOUNDATION, UK

INTRODUCTION

Picture the scene. A legion of new Year 7 students are excitedly beginning their first day at secondary school. Full of enthusiasm, they career from classroom to classroom, computer science to chemistry, French to food technology, eagerly absorbing new ideas and insights. However, for too many students, their interest will be quickly dimmed as they struggle to grapple with not just the language of French, but also with the challenging academic language of computer science and chemistry.

Consider this sobering fact for a moment. In 2019, only 73 per cent of students left primary school having reached the expected level for reading (DfE, 2019b). As a result of this reading barrier alone, students in most of our classrooms will therefore struggle to access the very language of school that attends the academic curriculum in secondary school. This evidence makes it clear, then, that literacy – and the explicit teaching of vocabulary, reading, writing, talk and listening – is not a bolt-on addition to our work, but an integral aspect of our daily teaching practice.

CHAPTER OBJECTIVES

By reading this chapter, you will understand:

- how to develop students' literacy by developing a repertoire for targeted vocabulary instruction;
- how to develop high-quality oral language in the classroom;
- the value of modelling in developing students' literacy skills.

An essential aspect of section 3 of the Early Career Framework (ECF) – on subject and curriculum – is the development of pupils' literacy. This is because our students' access to the curriculum is dependent upon their ability to read, write and talk using the academic code of school. By explicitly modelling the processes of being literate, such as using specialist academic vocabulary, we can best support our students to flourish and succeed in accessing the school curriculum.

THE ACADEMIC VOCABULARY NEEDED TO ACCESS THE CURRICULUM

To enable students to access the curriculum, they must first be literate in the specialist academic language of school. In secondary school, to think critically in a subject, you need a firm grasp of the specialist vocabulary in each subject domain. And so, in music, students need to access, and use, subject-specific vocabulary such as 'dynamics', 'harmony', 'texture', 'fortissimo' and 'pianissimo', whereas in science they need to understand and deploy 'photosynthesis', 'cracking', 'anhydrous', 'ester' and 'covalent bonding' with ease.

It is clear that the specialist academic language of each subject domain is not the same as the vocabulary we use in our daily conversation. The evidence is stark. Even children's books have 50 per cent more rare words than the conversation of graduates (Cunningham and Stanovich, 1998), not to mention the complexity of a science textbook. Given this evidence, we should consider how we can specifically target the teaching of academic vocabulary so that this crucial gateway to the curriculum is explicitly taught, not randomly caught by only a lucky few students.

Recently, a large-scale Oxford University Press teacher survey, involving over 1,000 teachers, showed that secondary school teachers judged as many as 43 per cent of Year 7 students did not have the vocabulary to access the school curriculum (Oxford University Press, 2018). Clearly, this vocabulary gap needs to be bridged. Though most of the words that students learn are acquired incidentally over time, via reading and similar, it is the highly specific vocabulary of the subject disciplines that most students won't grasp on an incidental basis. More explicit instruction of this vital literacy strand will be required.

It is first helpful to understand what we mean by academic vocabulary. US researchers William Nagy and Dianna Townsend have usefully defined six common features that describe typical academic language:

1.   A high proportion of Latin and Greek vocabulary.

2.   A high proportion of complex words that have complex spellings.

3.   A high proportion of nouns, adjectives and prepositions.

4.   A high proportion of expanded noun phrases and nominalisation.

5.   A high degree of informational density (i.e. few words that carry lots of meanings).

6.   A high degree of abstraction (i.e. words that are removed from the concrete here and now).

(Nagy and Townsend, 2012)

With scientific words such as 'photosynthesis' and 'anhydrous', we can see that they are of Greek origin. They are complex nouns that carry a lot of informational density. In simple terms, they are unfamiliar and hard words! Helpfully, with knowledge about word origins (etymology) and word parts (morphology), we can begin to access teaching strategies to help our students access these academic terms.

Consider what word roots are already familiar to you. 'Photo' – meaning light – and 'hydro' – meaning water – are both Greek word roots that most teachers can grasp, but all too often remain hidden to most of our students. When you add in 'syn' – meaning together – and 'an' – meaning 'without' – you actually help students recognise that the word parts offer concrete representations of these complex, seemingly abstract terms. This vocabulary strategy alone can help students access the language of school. Indeed, vocabulary offers us the bricks at the foundations of the school curriculum.

These common approaches to accessing academic words have a high utility for every teacher across different subject domains, given that a significant number of academic words we use in school have shared ancient Latin and Greek origins (Nagy and Townsend, 2012), with the proportion being as high as 90 per cent in areas of the curriculum such as maths and science (Green, 2008).

TARGETED VOCABULARY INSTRUCTION

In light of this evidence, consider a seemingly simple question: How do you teach a new word to your students?

Even for the most experienced of teachers, the difficulty that can arise from answering such a basic-seeming question can be chastening. Too much of the expert language of being a computer scientist, or a chemist, or a historian, can remain tacit, and this means that the students we teach who have a limited vocabulary more generally may not quite grasp the words that they need to ensure access to what is being taught in class.

You should avoid relying singularly on a dictionary to do the job for students. Consider how much knowledge is required of a word, its spelling as well as potential multiple meanings, to use a dictionary successfully. Instead of simply deferring to a dictionary, you should determine what academic words you need to plan to explicitly teach, utilising a range of strategies for explicit teaching.

Once we have selected the words to teach, we can then tackle explaining a new word. The following sequence is a handy guide to unpacking an academic term:

- Say the word carefully.

- Write the word (this offers opportunities to reference common sounds or letters in the word).

- Give a student-friendly definition (e.g. obtuse – not very sensitive or slow to understand).

- Give multiple meaningful examples (e.g. the prince was being deliberately obtuse).

- Ask for student examples and clarify multiple meanings or any misconceptions.

(adapted from Quigley, 2018, p140)

Despite our best-laid plans, it may be that words are thrown up mid-lesson that thwart our students. The aforementioned strategies still offer useful ways to tackle words that arise incidentally alongside a more deliberate and planned approach to developing vocabulary access to the entire academic curriculum.

> ## KEY QUESTIONS
>
> - What more do you need to know to understand your students' vocabulary knowledge and any gaps they may have upon entry to secondary school?
>
> - What is the vocabulary that is unique to your subject that proves essential knowledge for your students' progression?

THE IMPORTANCE OF HIGH-QUALITY TALK IN THE CLASSROOM

Talk is essential to communicate in the world and it is a potent tool for learning. High-quality talk underpins and can enhance other fundamental aspects of literacy such as reading and writing (Murphy et al., 2009).

High-quality talk is more likely to be structured and well organised – once more, taught and not merely caught. First, the teacher plays a role in modelling high-quality language use. This may include enhancing the vocabulary you use in explanations. For example, we use everyday words all the time to aid understanding, but we may recast our word choices to match a more academic register (e.g. 'sweat' may be recast as 'perspiration' in PE, 'or' may be recast as 'alternatively' in history). By establishing talk routines, including roles and goals for talk, you can create a rich platform to develop your students' understanding and help them access the curriculum.

Quality matters. As stated by the Education Endowment Foundation's *Improving Literacy in Secondary Schools* guidance report:

> *Quality of talk is likely to be more important than quantity. Improving quality means much more than getting students to talk more, or, as a teacher, trying to talk less. Instead, quality is more likely to be improved by considering structure and variety.*

> (EEF, 2018, p27)

You should, however, aim to go beyond students' merely reciting and imitating the language of the teacher to ensure discussion and extended dialogue is cultivated in the classroom (Alexander, 2017). Much research in the classroom has described the typical 'serve and return' of classroom talk between the teacher and student. Though question-and-answer sequences between the teacher and students in the class have their place, we can further the thinking of our students if we get them to elaborate on their ideas as well as those of their peers.

By deploying habitual talk routines in the classroom such as 'ABC feedback', we can encourage more developed dialogue on a daily basis in the classroom. ABC feedback is a shortcut, with 'A' representing 'agree with', 'B' representing 'build upon', and 'C' denoting 'challenge'. When faced with a big question such as 'What caused the decline of Motte-and-Bailey castles in England?' the ABC routine strategy can aid students in responding to one another's ideas. It militates against the simple get-out of 'I don't know' used so commonly by students.

KEY QUESTIONS

- What routines need to be established to ensure that students feel confident and able to engage in extended classroom talk?

- What strategies can be used to scaffold, extend and enrich talk of students in your classroom?

DEVELOPING QUESTIONING TO ENHANCE TALK

A key to developing the literacy of your students is to ensure that you ask carefully crafted questions that elicit insight and extend understanding. Given that teachers ask countless questions on a daily basis, small improvements in this aspect of teaching can aggregate and have a significant impact upon classroom practice more broadly.

Lots of enduring research has revealed that the mere act of asking a question can be mediated by how long students are given to think about the question posed. In research by Mary Budd Rowe as far back as the early 1970s, she revealed that teachers offer little more than a second to respond to a question (Rowe, 1972). This research on 'wait time' cuts at a fundamental habit we enact in the classroom. It can be hard to shift such ingrained habits. However, mere recognition of this fact – that a few more seconds of thinking time may significantly influence the quality of student talk – can help establish new habits to enhance classroom talk.

It is helpful to consider utilising a range of questions in the classroom. Researcher Angelo Cardiello offers a very useful categorisation of different question types:

- *Memory questions.* Who, what, when and where? For example, 'Who won the Battle of Hastings?'

- *Convergent thinking questions.* Who, how and in what way? Explaining relationships and cause/effect. For example, 'How did feminism develop in the twentieth century?'

- *Divergent thinking questions.* Imagine, predict, if-then questions. For example, 'How would Hamlet behave differently if he lived in modern-day England?'

- *Evaluative thinking questions.* Judge, justify and develop arguments. For example, 'Why did the German people become more nationalistic in the 1930s?'

(Ciardiello and Cicchell, 1994)

By integrating a more careful consideration of questioning, we begin to pay closer attention to the language used in the classroom. By sharpening this focus on this aspect of pedagogy and subject knowledge, we help attend to the literacy and language of our students and ensure that they access all aspects of the school curriculum.

KEY QUESTIONS

- What question types do you typically deploy in the classroom?

- What habits attending to wait time and questioning can we refine to increase the degree of high-quality talk in your classroom?

THE VITAL ROLE OF MODELLING IN THE CLASSROOM

It is clear that the language of the classroom is sophisticated and complex. The words we read, write and talk in daily life need to be mediated to match the academic demands of the school curriculum. We best teach the differences between reading, writing and talking in the different subject disciplines by modelling them for our students.

In secondary school, it is important to distinguish the nuanced subject differences which mean that we read like a chemist, talk like a computer scientist and write like a historian – termed 'disciplinary literacy' (Shanahan and Shanahan, 2012). For a teacher, it is manifested in small details, such as rereading a maths problem, writing a paragraph in history or explaining a process clearly in PE.

Once more, like developing vocabulary or asking questions, how we 'model' writing or talk in our classroom can too often remain tacit, given that it is seemingly 'natural'. For our most skilled students, they may appear to succeed with some natural flair, but for most students it is the deliberate – often slow – process of gradual improvement that is needed. Scaffolding students' understanding by modelling worked examples may offer us the prime vehicle to help our students move from novice status to experts in the subject discipline.

For example, in maths, a teacher may model a worked example for a given quadratic equation. This could then be followed by partial examples that students have to complete, with the teacher being explicit about possible next steps. Finally, the teacher may remove the scaffold and pose a sequence of different quadratic equations. A week later, it may be that the steps posed in the full worked example need to be reiterated. By foregrounding the strategies, we nudge our students to develop their metacognition (EEF, 2017) – that is to say, their ability to monitor their own thinking and choose the apt steps of a mathematician undertaking quadratic equations.

Just like an inexperienced teacher would watch a more experienced colleague, we need to ensure that we model subject expertise but also break it down into manageable steps. Many of the academic tasks in the classroom, such as writing an essay or designing a product, prove complex and overwhelming for novice students. Too often the subtle differences between accessing subject domains are not closely attended to and so students develop misconceptions. This can be at the level of uttering a fluent response in French that begins a more complex extended oral task, to writing a thesis statement to start a history essay.

KEY QUESTIONS

- What modelling methods do you currently deploy in the classroom? How deliberately and confidently do you enact this modelling?

- What aspects of talk, reading and writing could you model to better exemplify expertise in your subject discipline?

CONCLUSION

Talk develops how we think and learn. Reading is the gateway to the curriculum. Writing is our means to develop, evaluate and exemplify our understanding. In short, literacy is our students' gateway to the academic curriculum and the means for our students to succeed in school. It should then be beyond contention that every teacher should attend to disciplinary literacy.

As clearly stated in the ECF, 'Every teacher can improve pupils' literacy, including by explicitly teaching reading, writing and oral language skills specific to individual disciplines' (DfE, 2019a, p13).

We should consider the 'what' of curriculum development with great care. Crucially, however, we also need to attend to the 'how' of disciplinary literacy. By foregrounding this, we ensure that our students are not shut out by the specialist language of the school curriculum. Whether it is describing a musical score, reading a science textbook, or writing a geography case study, attending to literacy development will be beneficial to all, harmful to none, and essential for many of our students.

KEY CONCEPTS AND FURTHER READING

VOCABULARY INSTRUCTION AND HIGH-QUALITY ACADEMIC TALK

Education Endowment Foundation (EEF) (2018) *Improving Literacy in Secondary Schools*. Available at: https://educationendowmentfoundation.org.uk/public/files/Publications/Literacy/EEF_KS3_KS4_LITERACY_GUIDANCE.pdf

- This guidance report includes recommendations related to reading, writing, talk, vocabulary development and supporting struggling students.

DISCIPLINARY LITERACY

Shanahan, T. and Shanahan, C. (2012) What is disciplinary literacy and why does it matter? *Topics in Language Disorders*, 32(1): 7–18.

- This paper discusses the research base underlying disciplinary literacy.

MODELLING BY READING

Education Endowment Foundation (EEF) (2017) *Metacognition and Self-Regulation*. Available at: https://educationendowmentfoundation.org.uk/public/files/Publications/Metacognition/EEF_Metacognition_and_self-regulated_learning.pdf

- The third recommendation in this guidance report describes how to model your thinking.

REFERENCES

Alexander, R. (2017) *Towards Dialogic Teaching: Rethinking Classroom Talk*, 5th edn. York: Dialogos.

Ciardiello, A.V. and Cicchelli, T. (1994) The effects of instructional training models and content knowledge on student questioning in social studies. *The Journal of Social Studies Research*, 18(1): 30–7.

Cunningham, A.E. and Stanovich, K.E. (1998) What reading does for the mind. *American Educator*, 22(1–2): 8–15.

Department for Education (DfE) (2019a) *Early Career Framework*. London: DfE.

Department for Education (DfE) (2019b) *National Curriculum Assessments at Key Stage 2 in England, 2019 (Interim)*. Available at: www.gov.uk/government/publications/national-curriculum-assessments-key-stage-2-2019-interim/national-curriculum-assessments-at-key-stage-2-in-england-2019-interim

Education Endowment Foundation (EEF) (2017) *Metacognition and Self-Regulation*. Available at: https://educationendowmentfoundation.org.uk/public/files/Publications/Metacognition/EEF_Metacognition_and_self-regulated_learning.pdf

Education Endowment Foundation (EEF) (2018) *Improving Literacy in Secondary Schools*. Available at: https://educationendowmentfoundation.org.uk/public/files/Publications/Literacy/EEF_KS3_KS4_LITERACY_GUIDANCE.pdf

Green, T. (2008) *The Greek & Latin Roots of English*, 4th edn. Lanham, MD: Rowman & Littlefield.

Murphy, P., Wilkinson, I., Soter, A., Hennessey, M. and Alexander, J. (2009) Examining the effects of classroom discussion on students' comprehension of text: a meta-analysis. *Journal of Educational Psychology*, 101(3): 740–64.

Nagy, W. and Townsend, D. (2012) Words as tools: learning academic vocabulary as language acquisition. *Reading Research Quarterly*, 47(1): 91–108.

Oxford University Press (2018) *Why Closing the Word Gap Matters: Oxford Language Report*. Available at: http://fdslive.oup.com/www.oup.com/oxed/Oxford-Language-Report.PDF?region=uk

Quigley, A. (2018) *Closing the Vocabulary Gap*. London: Routledge.

Rowe, M.B. (1972) *Wait-Time and Rewards as Instructional Variables: Their Influence on Language, Logic and Fate Control*. Available at: https://files.eric.ed.gov/fulltext/ED061103.pdf

Shanahan, T. and Shanahan, C. (2012) What is disciplinary literacy and why does it matter? *Topics in Language Disorders*, 32(1): 7–18.

11

DEVELOPING LITERACY IN THE PRIMARY SCHOOL

MEGAN DIXON

DIRECTOR OF ENGLISH, ASPIRE EDUCATIONAL TRUST AND CO-DIRECTOR, ASPIRER
RESEARCH SCHOOL, CHESHIRE, UK

INTRODUCTION

Literacy matters more than we can possibly imagine – there is nothing that has more of an impact on the life chances of students than being able to read, write and speak with skill and confidence. By explicitly teaching reading, writing and oral language skills systematically, with attention to the process of learning, we can ensure that all students develop the skills they need to achieve their goals, to develop their knowledge and potential, and to participate effectively in society.

CHAPTER OBJECTIVES

This chapter introduces current thinking around some aspects of the development of literacy in the primary school to help you develop the skills and knowledge required to meet the relevant practice statements specified in sections 2, 3 and 4 of the Early Career Framework (ECF). With reference to the best available evidence, you will:

- learn about the importance of oral language development and explore the role of oracy for learning – you will consider the challenges children can face when developing language within an educational context and consider a number of effective strategies to support the development of oracy in the classroom;

(Continued)

(Continued)

- learn about developing vocabulary and some explicit strategies for teaching vocabulary in the classroom - you will understand the importance of vocabulary for literacy and the wider curriculum and consider how we can support students to acquire new vocabulary through explicit and implicit teaching;

- learn about the importance of scaffolding learning through a gradual release of responsibility when teaching to ensure learning of reading, writing and talk is as effective as possible.

It is difficult to separate the different aspects of literacy: the three cornerstones of language development, reading and writing are all interrelated and support each other. Of course, there is some core knowledge that students should acquire. This includes knowledge of letters, the ability to hear sounds in speech (phonological awareness) and relate different sounds to letters or groups of letters (phonics), and the understanding of spelling patterns and grammatical rules. These are tangible, discrete and measurable items of knowledge that are easily observed and assessed. Other aspects of literacy are harder to see and less obvious to measure – they involve the nuanced and subtle ways we communicate, either in speech or on paper. As teachers of literacy, we are teaching our students how to notice, how to predict, how to plan, how to monitor, how to comprehend, and how to evaluate our own spoken and written communications and those of others.

THE IMPORTANCE OF ORAL LANGUAGE DEVELOPMENT: THE ROLE OF ORACY FOR LEARNING

Spoken language is the foundation of literacy; without spoken language, there is no reading or writing. Some students will begin school with rich and well-developed vocabularies and a breadth of experience and knowledge on which to base their learning. Others will find the language used within school unfamiliar and intimidating and will not be as well placed to take advantage of the opportunities to learn in the classroom. Up to 10 per cent of our students will have language learning disorders (Norbury et al., 2016), making it challenging for them to access the curriculum successfully without careful, targeted and structured support.

Oracy, or the development of talk, should foster thinking, not simply require students to report on someone else's ideas. Students should learn how to pose their own questions and how to use talk to narrate, explain, speculate, imagine, hypothesise, explore, evaluate, discuss, argue, reason and justify (Alexander, 2012).

Language itself is developed by the serve and return of conversation – the amount of language a student hears is less important in comparison with the number of conversational turns they are involved in (Lieven et al., 2019). It is important to recognise that the language of text is different from the everyday language we use. We should be aware that different registers of talk are needed to achieve different communicative functions. This means that students need to learn to understand the difference in the style and tone of the language they use when they are speaking to their friends in the playground, explaining their writing to the head teacher, or in a formal debate. As teachers, we must model how we use language in different contexts and provide regular opportunities for students to use language and reflect on their own use of language.

WHAT HELPS WHEN DEVELOPING ORACY?

It is important to recognise that oracy is not just speaking; it is about using talk to promote and enhance learning – it is an end in itself, as well as the foundation for reading and writing. We can ensure our students develop their oracy skills effectively as follows:

1. *Ensuring talk is prioritised and being aware of our talk.* As teachers, we can explicitly model talk, using differing registers of talk within different situations and sharing with the children how we are using talk, and why.

2. *Teaching talk.* Teaching the language of negotiation, debate, discussion and narration. Using drama and role play provides the chance for students to use different registers of language and develop their self-regulation skills. Talking frames, sentence starters and the use of different roles within group work (perhaps using cooperative learning strategies) are all effective ways of scaffolding talk.

3. *Enriching talk.* Providing opportunities for students to use talk in a variety of ways and in differing contexts, including talk in small groups, talk to wider audiences (formal and informal), and questioning and responding.

4. *Noticing when talk is hard.* Being alert to the difficulties students might have in developing speech, language and communication skills, and becoming familiar with protocols and processes in your school for identifying and supporting children with language delay or language disorder.

KEY QUESTIONS

- Do you know what the normal developmental level of progression is for the development of speech, language and communication?

- How do you monitor and assess the development of a student's talk for learning?

- How do you model talk within the classroom? Do you model different registers (styles) of talk for your students to consider? How do you model talk for students with the other adults in your classroom and in school, and reflect on this to the students?

- How do you provide opportunities for your students to develop their talk skills and abilities?

TEACHING AND DEVELOPING VOCABULARY

There is evidence to suggest that developing vocabulary in our students in an attempt to narrow the word gap has a positive impact on a student's life chances (Asmussen et al., 2018; Law et al., 2017).

We cannot teach our students every word they will encounter in life; it is far more helpful to help them become interested in words – to be word-conscious. We can consider a knowledge of words from two different perspectives: a breadth of vocabulary and a depth of vocabulary. A breadth of vocabulary is considered to be the number of words a student knows; a depth of vocabulary describes the quality of their understanding of the words. Depth of vocabulary (i.e. understanding the meaning of the word, other words in the same family, words that mean the same, words that are different, words that sound the same) is more helpful for developing reading comprehension (Oakhill et al., 2015). Unless a student is familiar with the meaning, in context, of around 90 per cent of the words within a text, they will find it very difficult to understand the text with any depth of comprehension.

Teaching unfamiliar vocabulary explicitly and planning for pupils to be repeatedly exposed to high-utility and high-frequency vocabulary can be an effective and useful strategy. Words need words to be meaningful, so teaching lists of words in isolation, unrelated to a context or topic, is unlikely to be successful. Tier 2 words, also known as Goldilocks words or words that travel, are helpful words to teach (see Figure 11.1). These are words that have multiple meanings in differing contexts that students are likely to encounter regularly (see Beck et al., 2013).

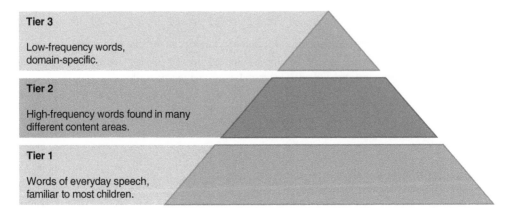

Figure 11.1   Tiers of vocabulary (EEF, 2018)

WHAT HELPS WHEN DEVELOPING VOCABULARY IN THE CLASSROOM?

1. *Explicitly drawing attention to words* when teaching helps students understand how to pay attention to words and the importance of using the right word at the right time. Help students notice when familiar words are used in different, unfamiliar contexts.

2. *Regular repeated exposure to words* is helpful. Be clear about the subject-specific vocabulary you use. Ensure that tier 2 words, or words that travel, are used and understood by all students.

3. *Pre-teaching vocabulary* before reading and writing and teaching words in semantic families helps students understand the nuanced differences between them. Help students explore how words sound (the phonology),

how words are written (the orthography), how words are constructed (the morphology) and how words are used (the semantic and syntactic contexts).

4. *Making links between reading and spelling words* has been shown to increase students' depth of understanding about words (Oakhill et al., 2015). It is helpful to teach students how words work – highlighting their morphology, their phonology and their orthography.

5. Ensure students are *celebrated for monitoring their own understanding of words* – build a culture in the classroom where it's OK not to know.

KEY QUESTIONS

- How do you explicitly introduce new vocabulary to students? What strategies do you use? How do you decide which words to focus on?

- How do you encourage your students to monitor their understanding of vocabulary and be word-conscious? How do they learn words for themselves?

- How do you make links between words in speech and in written text?

THE IMPORTANCE OF MODELLING

One of the greatest challenges in teaching reading and writing is to understand that we are teaching the processes of thinking involved in comprehending text and sharing our ideas. It is tempting to be seduced by the easily assessed aspects of literacy such as letter knowledge and spelling. The more nuanced aspects of composition and inferential understanding are harder to teach and harder to notice but are more powerful predictors of successful literacy acquisition if we teach them well.

One of the most effective means of teaching these ways of thinking about text is to model and think aloud while demonstrating how to read and write (Rosenshine, 2012). Teachers who think aloud, explaining the decisions they are making, are scaffolding to support students' learning. As students become more skilful, the scaffold can be gradually withdrawn – the teacher models only at points of difficulty, guiding contingently when needed.

We can use scaffolds in a variety of ways, such as explicitly modelling the thinking processes we are using and then providing a framework (e.g. template, working or completed example, planning tool) to enable the students to use that same thinking process. *Modelling* can be most effective in small groups, especially when teaching reading (EEF, 2019). A small group enables the teacher to carefully monitor and support the thinking of the students as they work and intervene at any point of difficulty.

It is important to remember that the end goal is for the student to be independent of the teacher, so we must always be planning to remove ourselves from the learning and provide opportunities for students to show us what they can do completely independently.

WHAT HELPS WHEN SCAFFOLDING LEARNING?

1. *Break the process down into smaller, manageable controllable steps*, remembering to practise the entire process, not just the individual steps. Use think-alouds to help students understand what and how to approach the thinking around the task.

2. *Use checklists, rubrics, worked examples, planning tools and thinking frameworks* to scaffold the process. Provide expert models and support them to complete each process independently.

3. *Ask students to think about when they are completing activities.* What aspects do they have under control? Where are the pinch points of misunderstanding? Encourage them to ask themselves, 'What have I done?' and 'What have I learnt?'

4. *Model reading comprehension.* Prompts such as 'who', 'why' and 'how' can help students learn to ask questions while they read. One example is the use of a technique called reciprocal reading, a dialogic method of supporting students to practise and internalise effective thought processes when they approach a text. It is most effectively used in small groups, with the teacher supporting the students to use the four thinking approaches of predicting, questioning, clarifying and summarising in a reflective discussion (EEF, 2019).

5. *Model the writing process.* Teach the process of writing explicitly by modelling each stage: planning, goal-setting, drafting, editing, revising and evaluating (EEF, 2017a).

Encourage students to write for multiple audiences and purposes and provide regular and extensive shared, guided and independent opportunities to write.

KEY QUESTIONS

- How do you explicitly model the process of comprehending a text? Do you model this in a wide variety of contexts and across a range of texts and subject areas?

- How do you explicitly model the process of writing? Do you model this in a wide variety of contexts and across a range of texts?

- How do you monitor your students' understanding of text or the process of writing?

- What opportunities do you provide for your students to work completely independently and reflect on their learning?

CONCLUSION

Central to every aspect of literacy is the importance of oral language development. We must be skilled at identifying and supporting children with specific language difficulties, in addition to supporting and developing talk for learning – oracy. The use of words is central to talk. But words are only useful when they are surrounded by other words – context matters. We can support students by encouraging them to become word-conscious. Building on this, the pedagogies of thinking aloud and scaffolding enables children to gradually become more independent and able to communicate in an increasingly clear and sophisticated way.

We must pay total attention to explicitly teaching reading, writing and oral language skills systematically, with attention to the process of learning. Only by doing this can we ensure that all students develop the skills they need to achieve their goals, to develop their knowledge and potential, and to participate effectively in society.

Nothing matters more.

KEY CONCEPTS AND FURTHER READING

LITERACY

The Education Endowment Foundation guidance reports on improving literacy at Key Stage 1 (EEF, 2017b) and Key Stage 2 (EEF, 2017c) explore the evidence base for developing literacy in primary schools. Each report is heavily referenced, with links easily available on the EEF website (**https://educationendowmentfoundation.org.uk**).

ORACY

Professor Robin Alexander's website includes resources and tools for teachers: **https://robinalexander.org.uk/dialogic-teaching/**

Oracy at Cambridge offers resources and materials to support you in developing talk in your classroom: **https://languageresearch.cambridge.org/images/Language_Research/CambridgePapers/CambridgePapersInELT_Oracy_2018.pdf**

Voice 21 – The Oracy Benchmarks: **https://voice21.org/wp-content/uploads/2019/11/Benchmarks-report.pdf**

VOCABULARY

Although not written for the English context, *Bringing Words to Life* (Beck et al., 2013) is the seminal text on vocabulary and is drawn from extensive research and practical experience in supporting vocabulary growth in schools.

Pre-Teach Vocabulary by Pip St John is a free resource to support teachers with the development of vocabulary in the classroom: **https://pipstjohn.files.wordpress.com/2016/10/pre-teaching-vocabulary-pip-st-john-oct-2016.pdf**

SCAFFOLDING READING AND WRITING

Graham, S. (2019) Changing how writing is taught. *Review of Research in Education*, 43(1): 277–303.

Ricketts, J. and Dixon, M. (2018) *Going to Bat for the Neglected Art of Comprehension*. Available at: www.tes.com/magazine/article/going-bat-neglected-art-comprehension

REFERENCES

Alexander, R. (2012) *Improving Oracy and Classroom Talk in English Schools: Achievements and Challenges*. Available at: http://eprints.whiterose.ac.uk/76321/1/R_alexander_improving_oracy.pdf

Asmussen, K., Law, J., Charlton, J., Acquah, D., Brims, L., Pote, I., et al. (2018) *Key Competencies in Early Cognitive Development: Things, People, Numbers and Words*. Available at: www.eif.org.uk/report/key-competencies-in-early-cognitive-development-things-people-numbers-and-words

Beck, I., McGeown, M. and Lucan, L. (2013) *Bringing Words to Life*, 2nd edn. New York: Guilford Press.

Education Endowment Foundation (EEF) (2017a) *Improving Secondary Science Guidance Report*. Available at: https://educationendowmentfoundation.org.uk/public/files/Support/Publications/Science/EEF_improving_secondary_science.pdf

Education Endowment Foundation (EEF) (2017b) *Improving Literacy at KS1 Guidance Report*. Available at: https://educationendowmentfoundation.org.uk/public/files/Support/Publications/Literacy/KS1_Literacy_Guidance_2017.pdf

Education Endowment Foundation (EEF) (2017c) *Improving Literacy at KS2 Guidance Report*. Available at: https://educationendowmentfoundation.org.uk/public/files/Support/Publications/Literacy/KS2_Literacy_Guidance_2017.pdf

Education Endowment Foundation (EEF) (2018) *Preparing for Literacy: Improving Communication, Language and Literacy in the Early Years*. Available at: https://educationendowmentfoundation.org.uk/public/files/Publications/Literacy/Preparing_Literacy_Guidance_2018.pdf

Education Endowment Foundation (EEF) (2019) *Reciprocal Reading: Evaluation Report*. Available at: https://educationendowmentfoundation.org.uk/public/files/Projects/Evaluation_Reports/Reciprocal_Reading.pdf

Law, J., Charlton, J., Dockrell, J., Gascoigne, M., McKean, C. and Theakston, A. (2017) Early language development: needs, provision, and intervention for preschool children from socioeconomically disadvantaged backgrounds, a report for the Education Endowment Foundation. Available at: https://educationendowment-foundation.org.uk/public/files/Law_et_al_Early_Language_Development_final.pdf

Lieven, E., Theakston, A. and Rowland, C. (2019) *Quantity vs Quality of Child-Directed Speech: Which Matters Most?* Available at: www.lucid.ac.uk/media/2066/quantity-vs-quality.pdf

Norbury, C.F., Gooch, D., Wray, C., Baird, G., Charman, T., Simonoff, E., et al. (2016) The impact of nonverbal ability on prevalence and clinical presentation of language disorder: evidence from a population study. *Journal of Child Psychology and Psychiatry and Allied Disciplines*, 57(11): 1247–57.

Oakhill, J., Cain, K. and Elbro, C. (2015) *Understanding and Teaching Reading Comprehension: A Handbook*. New York: Routledge.

Rosenshine, B. (2012) Principles of instruction: research-based strategies that all teachers should know. *American Educator*, 36(1): 12–19.

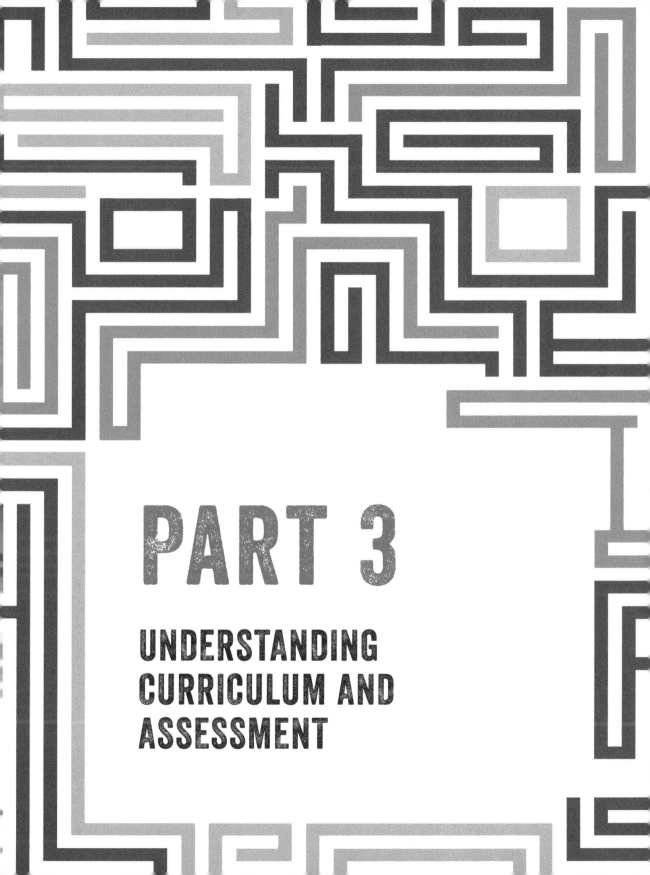

PART 3

UNDERSTANDING CURRICULUM AND ASSESSMENT

12

PRINCIPLES OF ASSESSMENT

SARAH EARLE

BATH SPA UNIVERSITY, BATH, UK

INTRODUCTION

This chapter is focused on the principles behind assessment in the classroom. It might not always feel like it, but as teachers we are constantly using assessment information to make decisions about what to say, what task to set, what to do with task outcomes and what to do next. Every interaction with students is a potential assessment opportunity, not in the sense of end-of-year judgements, but in the sense that the interaction can provide us with information about how the learning is going, in order to help us to adapt our teaching.

Assessment influences school and classroom culture, impacts on pupil and teacher ideas about learning, and determines what is taught and how. According to Stobart (2008), 'Assessment does not objectively measure what is already there, but rather creates and shapes what is measured' (p1). The taught curriculum is driven by assessment requirements; thus, developing an in-depth understanding of assessment, or 'teacher assessment literacy', is essential in the move from novice to expert teacher.

The Early Career Framework (ECF) seeks to 'support all pupils to succeed' (DfE, 2019, p4), and the effective use of assessment provides both the means to identify whether students have succeeded together with the information to help teachers support those who have not yet 'got there'. Section 6 requires the 'accurate and productive use' of assessment (DfE, 2019, p19). This chapter will emphasise the 'use' of assessment as we consider principles and purposes.

CHAPTER OBJECTIVES

In this chapter, you will learn about four key concepts:

- *formative* and *summative* purposes to support meaningful use of assessment;
- the principles of *validity* and *reliability* to inform your decision-making.

FORMATIVE AND SUMMATIVE PURPOSES TO SUPPORT MEANINGFUL USE OF ASSESSMENT

In its broadest sense, assessment is an integral part of teaching that includes 'the process of gathering, interpreting and using evidence to make judgements about students' achievements' (Harlen, 2007, p11). This could be part of normal classroom activities or a special task. All interactions with students potentially provide information that could support the teacher to make judgements. To broaden this idea even further, the student themselves should be included as a potential judgement-maker, involving them in the active monitoring of their own learning.

The purpose of an assessment is often hard to define, with information being used by a range of people for a variety of reasons. An important classification concerns formative and summative purposes. Before exploring each in turn, it is important to note that it is the use, rather than the activity, which designates the categorisation, because the majority of tasks can be utilised for formative or summative purposes. For example, a multiple-choice quiz can be used formatively to diagnose gaps in understanding or summatively to check understanding at the end of a unit.

FORMATIVE PURPOSE IN PRACTICE

The terms 'formative' and 'assessment for learning' (AfL) are used largely interchangeably to mean assessment information that is used to support learning: 'Assessment provides information ... Such assessment becomes "formative assessment" when the evidence is actually used to adapt the teaching work to meet the needs' (Black and Wiliam, 1998, p2). Formative assessment concerns the ongoing classroom assessment practices that inform your teaching. This could be something that you do at the beginning of a topic to inform your planning for the term, or it might be something you do within the lesson to check whether students need more time on a concept or if they are ready to move on. Within lessons, opportunities for formative assessment can benefit from consideration in advance (e.g. deciding on key or 'hinge-point' questions, the focus for student recording).

Black and Wiliam (2009) identified the following aspects of formative assessment (which are considered in more detail in Wiliam, 2018):

- where the learner is going – clarifying learning intentions and criteria for success;

- where the learner is right now – eliciting evidence of student understanding through questioning, discussion and other learning tasks;

- how to get there – providing feedback that moves the learner forward;

- utilising peer and self-assessment.

These aspects could act as a guide for teachers to prompt reflection on classroom practice and help select which element could be the focus for professional development. For example, if a teacher finds that their questioning is not providing useful information about student understanding, then they may explore ways to increase the 'wait time' to provide the opportunity for more in-depth discussion and more detailed replies (Black et al., 2004, p12). The aspects listed above are general principles rather than specifics for each lesson, because formative assessment is not a list of strategies or a 'recipe' to follow; it requires ongoing reflection within and about the lesson. Responsive teachers utilise their pedagogical content knowledge (PCK) to develop and refine interactions with their students to support their learning.

The pupils are giving you feedback about their learning in each verbal or written interaction. When you have identified a need, a gap or a misconception (also called alternative conceptions), then the key to formative assessment is to make sure you do something with the information – be responsive in your teaching. For example, you might:

- ask the question in a different way to support understanding;

- provide an additional explanation or demonstration;

- make a note of a tricky concept to address in a later lesson;

- identify those pupils who need some extra support in a particular area;

- give verbal feedback to be acted upon in the lesson;

- direct pupils to the agreed success criteria to support their peer and self-assessment.

KEY QUESTIONS

- Which strategies could you use more or less?

- What ways can we make formative assessment more efficient (e.g. time to act on feedback within the lesson)?

SUMMATIVE PURPOSE IN PRACTICE

The purpose of summative assessment is to report or summarise attainment at a particular point in time. This could be at a key point during or at the end of a year but is not the same as 'tracking'. Tracking is the recording of pupil progress data, but before the data are entered a judgement has been made. The means of judgement needs to be taken into account when deciding on the meaning and trust in the tracking data. We will return to the issue of trust when discussing validity and reliability below.

Summative assessment might be based on a 'snapshot' – an activity at a particular point in time, such as an end-of-term test or a 'summary' that takes a range of information into account such as an end-of-Key Stage teacher assessment (Earle, 2019). Utilising a wide range of information when drawing conclusions, 'by looking at patterns of performance over a number of assessments' (DfE, 2019, p19), can help us to have more confidence in our judgements, because we are less likely to be focusing on results that are context- or task-dependent. Nevertheless, if all of the assessment tasks are drawn from the same pool, or of the same type, then we may still want to consider how much trust we place in our judgements. For example, written assessments for young children, where many of the class cannot yet read fluently, may only tell us about their reading attainment rather than any knowledge of the topic.

Decisions about purposeful summative assessment should be directly related to the primary aim of reporting or summarising attainment. With this in mind, it is useful to consider the audience. Who is the report or summary for? Identifying the audience will help to decide the amount of detail and the language to be used, since this will vary depending on whether the report is for a pupil, other staff (e.g. next teacher, head of department, etc.), parents, and so on. Nevertheless, assessment that has a primarily summative purpose can still be used in a formative way (e.g. identify gaps to inform the next term's planning). Teachers may use summative assessment information over a longer period of time to support development of their practice or the school's curriculum.

The competing uses of assessment can place the teacher in a 'conflicted position' (Green and Oates, 2009, p233). Assessment for accountability may seemingly require a different approach to using assessment as part of the learning process. When feeling this 'conflict', a discussion with colleagues could be useful to clarify the purpose of the assessment. Teacher assessment literacy is an ongoing and developmental process (DeLuca et al., 2016) that will continue throughout your career, and such collaborative reflection can be useful for all colleagues. When considering assessment, formative or summative, the key point is to consider how the information will be used, since if the information is of little use, then there is little point in the assessment activity.

KEY QUESTIONS

Assessment information can be utilised for a wide range of purposes, such as diagnosis, monitoring of progress, next steps, grouping, reporting, gap analysis, selection, accountability, and supporting learning.

- Which of these purposes are formative and/or summative?

- What do you use assessment for in your classroom?

THE PRINCIPLES OF VALIDITY AND RELIABILITY TO INFORM YOUR DECISION-MAKING

When making decisions about what assessment task to do, or what information to gather, a consideration of the principles of validity and reliability can be of assistance. Both validity and reliability can be examined in great depth; to keep our discussion focused on the classroom, a brief definition for each is presented here, before discussing each in turn:

- *Validity*: Whether an assessment is fit for purpose and actually assesses what we want it to – does it merit the inferences we base on it?

- *Reliability*: Trust in accuracy or consistency of an assessment.

VALIDITY

Construct validity concerns how well the assessment samples the underlying skill, concept or subject (Stobart, 2009). When deciding on an assessment activity, it is important to consider what you would like to know: which knowledge, understanding or skills should be the focus? Recognising that an assessment activity can only sample a small part of the curriculum, it is worth confirming which part you are wanting to know about (not just the part that is easy to check!). This will help to decide if the task is fit for your purpose (Green and Oates, 2009) and whether your inferences based on the results are justified. For example, a times table test can support inferences about a child's recall of multiplication facts, but not about the child's attainment in mathematical problem-solving. Checking whether our inferences are justified helps to challenge our preconceived assumptions about our students. We all have such preconceived assumptions, which help to make our teaching more manageable; we plan our lessons by second-guessing what students will be able to do, but assessment helps us to check whether they were able to do it or not.

Two threats to validity are useful to consider when exploring the validity of assessment judgements. 'Construct under-representation' is the name given to issues of limited sampling of the subject, when the assessment is only focused on a small part of what you are interested in. For example, if only the decoding of words is assessed for reading, comprehension of the text will be under-represented. To alleviate this threat, you need to either broaden the assessment information (e.g. broader task, utilising more tasks over time) or limit your inferences to more limited judgements about the sample assessed. The second threat to validity is 'construct-irrelevance', whereby something gets in the way of the thing you are trying to assess, such as if the maths questions were too hard to read, or marking is focused more on the neatness of the handwriting than the historical enquiry skills that were the focus for the assessment. Being very clear about the objective(s) being assessed helps to alleviate this threat to validity.

This discussion links to the question of whether the assessment is considering learning or merely performance. For example, has the pupil said the right word to get the mark, even if they have not understood it? One student supplying a correct answer for the class may be a 'poor proxy for learning' (Coe, 2013, p12). We can only assess the behaviours we see, so we are reliant on performance to a certain extent. However, by drawing on a range of information and by discussing and questioning further, we can be more confident in our judgements. For example, if they use the right word, does that mean they understand? You may need to question further or ask them to explain. Do they need to 'say it' just once? You may need to ask them to demonstrate their learning on more than one occasion (e.g. revisiting the topic later in the term).

RELIABILITY

Reliability concerns the trust we have in the accuracy or consistency of an assessment (Mansell et al., 2009), such as whether we would expect a similar result if we had asked the questions on a different day, or if we trust the assessment enough to be able to compare between groups (if we need to). This is not just an afterthought; if we do not need to compare with other groups, in particular when we are using assessment formatively, then reliability is less of a concern. If the assessment is primarily about supporting students' learning, then sitting the task in comparable conditions, for example, is not a priority. Reliability should be more of a concern for assessments with a primarily summative purpose.

Reliability issues can be split into internal and external. Internal reliability concerns the task itself, such as whether the wording of questions are clear enough to mean the same to everyone, since there may be terms that are reliant on previous knowledge, which could disadvantage some. External reliability concerns issues outside of the task, such as marker consistency, which concerns whether other markers agree with your judgement. In situations where it is important to reach agreement, lists of criteria or mark schemes might be developed. These can help markers to be consistent, but they may also narrow the indicators to a point where the assessment is more about ticking boxes than student attainment. For example, Key Stage 2 English writing assessment tick lists arguably led to a focus on grammatical devices rather than coherent purposeful writing, with new methods of 'comparative judgement' now being explored (e.g. **www.nomoremarking.com**) as a holistic alternative to criteria lists.

Reliability can be strengthened by:

- clearly defined criteria (e.g. success criteria, mark schemes, national curriculum or exam board objectives);

- external materials in controlled conditions (if end-of-year/Key Stage assessments need to be compared across groups);

- standardisation (e.g. compare work to agree the standard);

- moderation, which may include standardisation, but also broader discussions about what 'meeting' and progression look like.

A final point regarding validity and reliability is that they can appear to be at odds with each other: 'an assessment cannot have both high validity and high reliability' (Harlen, 2007, p23). It is not possible to have highly repeatable, standardised assessment that samples the whole of the subject. Reliability relies on narrowing the task to help markers agree, while validity depends on the opposite: as broad a sampling of the subject as possible. This can be seen as an 'inevitable trade-off' (Wiliam, 2003) or a balancing act (Earle, 2017). The aim is to be reliable enough for the purpose, hence the need to be clear about the purpose of the assessment. For example, for primarily formative assessment, the support of learning is more important than standardised conditions, while a snapshot summative task for comparison across the cohort will need to address concerns of reliability.

KEY QUESTIONS

Consider an assessment you have set for your students.

- Was it fit for purpose? Did it assess what you wanted it to? (*validity*)

- How accurate do you think it was? Would others agree? (*reliability*)

CONCLUSION

This chapter has discussed the key concepts of formative and summative assessment as well as validity and reliability, which are briefly summarised in this final section. Further considerations include manageability, impact and value. In short, we are asking: *Is it worth it?* The assessment needs to be manageable, to fit within the time constraints of the lesson and teacher workload. The assessment needs to provide value and useful information that can be put to use to impact the learning of individuals or cohorts.

At first glance, it may appear that we just need to 'get on with it' when it comes to assessment, with statutory and school structures guiding practice. But as discussed in this chapter, assessment is an integral part of your teaching and you can make decisions about its implementation and use on a daily basis. Pausing for reflection on assessment practice can help us to make assessment opportunities more fruitful and our teaching more responsive.

KEY CONCEPTS AND FURTHER READING

FORMATIVE PURPOSE: ASSESSMENT THAT AIMS TO DIRECTLY SUPPORT STUDENT LEARNING

Black, P., Harrison, C., Lee, C., Marshall, B. and Wiliam, D. (2004) Working inside the black box: assessment for learning in the classroom. *Phi Delta Kappan*, 86(1): 8–21.

- This is an accessible overview of formative assessment.

TEACHER ASSESSMENT LITERACY

Mansell, W., James, M. and the Assessment Reform Group (2009) *Assessment in Schools: Fit for Purpose?* London: Teaching and Learning Research Programme.

- This is a useful open-access discussion of assessment challenges.

VALIDITY AND RELIABILITY

Earle, S. (2017) 'But I've not got time for any more assessment': balancing the demands of validity and reliability. *Impact*, 1(1): 44–6.

- This article further discusses validity and reliability.

REFERENCES

Black, P. and Wiliam, D. (1998) *Inside the Black Box*. London: GL Assessment.

Black, P. and Wiliam, D. (2009) Developing the theory of formative assessment. *Educational Assessment, Evaluation and Accountability*, 21(1): 5–31.

Black, P., Harrison, C., Lee, C., Marshall, B. and Wiliam, D. (2004) Working inside the black box: assessment for learning in the classroom. *Phi Delta Kappan*, 86(1): 8–21.

Coe, R. (2013) *Improving Education: A Triumph of Hope over Experience*. Available at: www.cem.org/attachments/publications/ImprovingEducation2013.pdf

DeLuca, C., LaPointe-McEwan, D. and Luhanga, U. (2016) Approaches to classroom assessment inventory: a new instrument to support teacher assessment literacy. *Educational Assessment*, 21(4): 248–66.

Department for Education (DfE) (2019) *Early Career Framework*. London: DfE.

Earle, S. (2017) 'But I've not got time for any more assessment': balancing the demands of validity and reliability. *Impact*, 1(1): 44–6.

Earle, S. (2019) *Assessment in the Primary Classroom: Principles and Practice*. London: Learning Matters.

Green, S. and Oates, T. (2009) Considering the alternatives to national assessment arrangements in England: possibilities and opportunities. *Educational Research*, 51(2): 229–45.

Harlen, W. (2007) *Assessment of Learning*. London: SAGE.

Mansell, W., James, M. and the Assessment Reform Group (2009) *Assessment in Schools: Fit for Purpose?* London: Teaching and Learning Research Programme.

Stobart, G. (2008) *Testing Times: The Uses and Abuses of Assessment*. London: Routledge.

Stobart, G. (2009) Determining validity in national curriculum assessments. *Educational Research*, 51(2): 161–79.

Wiliam, D. (2003) National curriculum assessment: how to make it better. *Research Papers in Education*, 18(2): 129–36.

Wiliam, D. (2018) *Embedded Formative Assessment*, 2nd edn. Bloomington, IN: Solution Tree Press.

13

GAUGING UNDERSTANDING AND IDENTIFYING MISCONCEPTIONS

NIKI KAISER

CHEMISTRY TEACHER AND NETWORK RESEARCH LEAD, NOTRE DAME HIGH SCHOOL, NORWICH, UK

INTRODUCTION

The Earth goes around the Sun, doesn't it? We all know this, don't we? But deep down, do you really believe this? As you observe the Sun rising in the east every morning, appearing to cross the sky from one side to the other, and setting in the west, it feels counter-intuitive to think that we're standing on the body that's orbiting the other. This concept helps you to understand other things, such as why we have days and years, but how would you know it if someone hadn't told you?

This chapter is about misconceptions: how and why they exist, how we know which misconceptions our students hold, why it's important to challenge them, and how we know if and when they've truly overcome them.

This chapter relates to Parts 1–3 of section 6 in the Early Career Framework (ECF), 'Assessment', which outlines how effective assessment is critical because it allows you to plan and adapt your teaching to respond to your students' needs. Without assessment, you are limited to poor proxies for learning, such as how busy your students are or how much they've written, both of which indicate your students' current performance rather than how much they'll retain in the long term.

In this chapter, you will read about anticipating and planning for common misconceptions, and how you might diagnose the misconceptions that students hold. You'll be prompted to think about how you might respond to them, and how you'll know if your students have overcome them. These are key to teaching and learning because if you don't know what your students know and think, you're metaphorically teaching in the dark, with little idea of what you should do and why.

CHAPTER OBJECTIVES

In this chapter, you will learn about:

- the relationship between learning and misconceptions;

- planning for misconceptions;

- assessing students' understanding;

- responding to misconceptions.

LEARNING AND MISCONCEPTIONS

Your students will have developed many beliefs or preconceptions during their childhoods; some, but not all, will align with what they learn at school. For simplicity, the word 'misconception' is used here for any belief or misunderstanding that is likely to hinder your students' understanding of more complex ideas, which might include preconceptions or alternative conceptions.

You should plan around what your students are likely to find confusing by anticipating, diagnosing and addressing their likely misconceptions. To do this, you will need to know about the common misconceptions in your area before you begin teaching, and find out what your students believe before, during and after your teaching.

PRIOR KNOWLEDGE

It's not unusual to teach a seemingly excellent lesson, where you've answered everyone's questions fully and picked robust examples to back up your point, yet when you check through students' work afterwards, discover that they've understood something completely different to the point you were trying to make. There will often be several different individual conceptions of the same idea in any class.

This is because the way we assimilate and conceptualise new ideas is strongly influenced by what we already know. So, if you were a child in the 1980s and you hear the 1812 Overture, for example, it might make you think about a peanut butter advert that used it as background music, whereas other people might know its historical context, and others will just think it's a catchy piece of classical music. Similarly, if a student learns that Ursa Major is called 'the Plough', it'll make no sense to them if they've never seen a plough before, although they might think it looks like a saucepan. And if you use the flow of water through heating pipes to try to help explain current in circuits, it won't help students who have limited knowledge of central heating systems.

Different students will take their own meaning from everything you teach because their individual prior knowledge and beliefs will influence what they understand (or misunderstand). But as they learn, they will build knowledge networks (or schemas) in their long-term memory and make connections with things they already know. The more prior knowledge they've embedded, the more connections they can make, and the more complex (and useful) these networks become. So, you will have a greater chance of connecting to students' prior knowledge when using analogies and examples, if you use as many as you can, rather than sticking to a single model that makes sense to you.

According to the ECF, 'learning involves a lasting change in pupils' ... understanding', and it's easy to think of this only in terms of remembering more (DfE, 2019, p10). But in the context of misconceptions, our students need to develop (and sometimes forget) existing ideas to accommodate new ones. To support them to do this, you need to know what your students know and think, which is why we use assessment.

KEY QUESTIONS

- Have you encountered any unexpected prior beliefs among your students? Are there any that were particularly prevalent?

- Can you think of a time when your students took a completely different meaning from something than you expected them to?

Try reading insight 8 in McCrea (2009) to find out more.

PLANNING FOR MISCONCEPTIONS

When you are planning a sequence of lessons, it's useful to know the misconceptions that students might already hold about the area, and the ones that tend to develop as they learn more. If you can anticipate these, you can plan how you'll help your students to navigate them and think about how you'll know if they've understood everything afterwards.

Misconceptions might arise because:

- something feels logical (e.g. copper atoms are red but chlorine atoms are green);

- we try to simplify things for our students (e.g. use a comma to show where the reader should take a breath);

- students have an incomplete understanding of something (e.g. adding an apostrophe to any word ending in 's');

- it appears to be common sense (e.g. people live near volcanoes because it's cheaper);

- students pick them up through everyday experience (e.g. Vikings wore horns on their helmets).

However they arise, they should be uncovered so you can challenge them and help your students to understand why they're unhelpful.

SOURCES OF HELP

As you teach, you'll build up a bank of knowledge about the common hurdles in your subject, although this will take time. But you can find out about the misconceptions that your students are likely to hold in other ways, as follows:

- Completing the work yourself beforehand:

    o   If you answer the question, do the calculation, carry out the activity or plan the essay that you plan to set for your students, it can help you to pre-empt the likely hurdles that students will encounter.

    o   The drawback to this approach is that it's not always easy to appreciate what will be tricky for a novice to grasp, because many things that your students struggle with will be second nature to you.

- Asking other teachers for pointers:

    o   Experienced teachers will be familiar with issues that occur repeatedly.

    o   Take advantage of any structured departmental planning sessions to use colleagues' ideas and experience around students' misconceptions, and plan together how you might help students overcome them.

- Keeping a note of any misconceptions you encounter as you teach:

    o   This will give you a head start the next time you teach this topic.

    o   You can find information about common misconceptions from a variety of sources, such as textbooks, examiner reports or subject-specific collections such as the AAAS assessment bank for science (**assessment.aaas.org/topics**).

Plan how you'll take account of the common misconceptions you find in any future explanations. Use stories that highlight them for your students, if you can, as they tend to draw students in and help them to remember (Willingham, 2004), and use a range of examples and analogies.

KEY QUESTIONS

- Pick a common misconception for an upcoming topic and think about how and when it is likely to surface. How will you take account of it in your planning?

- Use textbooks or other literature to find other common misconceptions for an upcoming topic.

ASSESSING UNDERSTANDING

Teaching would be so much easier if we could look inside our students' heads and see what they were really thinking. But we can't, so we need to find ways of probing their thoughts, to find out what they think and why. This is why assessment is such an important aspect of teaching and learning.

Assessment is a broad term, encompassing a range of approaches, from verbal questions to written homework. It doesn't (necessarily) refer to formal tests, and could be as straightforward as a conversation or a glance at a child's book during a lesson. The key point is that however these tasks and questions are delivered, they should enable you to identify gaps in students' knowledge and any prevailing misconceptions.

If you're going to challenge your students' misconceptions, they first need to be brought to the surface, so it's important to strive for a classroom culture where your students feel comfortable to share their thinking. Let them know that everyone holds misconceptions – even famous scientists and great philosophers. Learning involves people changing and developing their ideas, otherwise we'd all still think that the Earth is flat!

A straightforward way of eliciting students' misconceptions is simply to prompt them to elaborate on their ideas when you're talking to them, so you can check whether or not correct answers stem from secure understanding. You can also use more structured forms of assessment, asking focused questions that home in on a particular point.

Think ahead about the kinds of responses that would indicate understanding, and plan how you will respond to those students that need further support. Make sure you use assessment to find out what your students actually know, rather than just testing them to reassure yourself or contribute to data collection. Plan assessment around your learning objectives, and use it to uncover any misconceptions before, during and after you teach.

DIAGNOSTIC ASSESSMENT

Diagnostic questions are designed to help you find out what your students are thinking so you can decide on your next steps. Good diagnostic questions concentrate on a specific learning point, enabling you to check if everyone in the class understands, and to find out which students are struggling. They also allow you to draw out thoughts from less vocal students so you can give them timely feedback.

You can use diagnostic questions to check on students' prior knowledge at the start of a topic, or later, at a key point in a learning sequence, to review understanding and help you to decide when and how to move on. Questions such as this (often called hinge-point questions) should ideally take no more than a couple of minutes for students to respond to, and you should be able to interpret responses immediately, so that you can quickly decide how to respond to them (Wiliam, 2011). Multiple-choice questions are very useful for this.

Good multiple-choice questions use common misconceptions as distractors, so you can quickly see which ones are held by your students, and are easy for your students to interpret. You want to be certain that your students' responses are based on their understanding of the underlying concept rather than how easily they can read or decode a question.

Questions such as this could be completed individually or in small groups (to encourage discussion), and you can present questions and responses in words or as pictures, so you can adapt them to the particular context in which you're working. Getting the class to vote on the correct answer will give you immediate information about what the class is thinking, which can be as simple as students indicating their response on their fingers, or with any technology you tend to use.

You could project a question on to the board and give the class ten seconds' thinking time, before giving them a countdown to display their answers at the same time, or even ask students to close their eyes and put their hands up when you make a statement they agree with, so you can get an immediate idea of individual students' thinking. However you carry it out, your assessment should be efficient and take little time away from the rest of the lesson.

KEY QUESTIONS

- How often do you check for understanding before moving on? When and how could you do this? Think of the 'hinge points' in an upcoming topic, where you'll need to check that everyone has understood a key point before moving on. This video, where Dylan Wiliam describes hinge-point questions, might help you to frame your ideas: **www.youtube.com/watch?v=Mh5SZZt2O7k**

- Explore this bank of diagnostic questions to find questions you might use in an upcoming topic: **https://diagnosticquestions.com/learn**

RESPONDING TO MISCONCEPTIONS

Once you've found out what your students think, you'll need to decide how to support them if needed. The way you do this will depend, to a certain extent, on the timing of the assessment. At the start of a topic, you may be able to plan around them, but later in a topic you might need to give certain students further support to understand something, give further examples or practice tasks, or even reteach something.

Whether you divert the course of a lesson from the one you originally planned, or find you have to change a future lesson to take these misconceptions into account, you will need to allow time to do so. This can feel difficult to justify when you are conscious that you want to teach everything in whatever time you have. However, time spent at an early stage should save you time later, because these misconceptions would have to have been unpicked later anyway, and by then they would have been even more entrenched.

It's also worth remembering that you might actually find out your students understand something better than you suspected they might, allowing you to move on more quickly than you'd originally expected.

Once you've uncovered any misconceptions, you'll want to challenge them. But your students are likely to need to see compelling evidence for changing their thinking, and one way of doing this is to provide them with evidence that conflicts with their ideas. This could be through a structured process, such as the Cognitive Acceleration through Science Education (CASE) programme, or in a less formalised way, by planning your lesson in a way that deliberately forces students to interrogate their own ideas.

It would make life easy if your students could remember new concepts indefinitely once they'd learnt them, but they will often appear to 'unlearn' them afterwards. Shtulman and Valcarcel (2012) argued that we can only ever hope to suppress previously held misconceptions, and Nuthall (2007) suggested that students will probably need to encounter ideas on at least three occasions before they really learn them; experience will tell you that ideas take time to sink in.

It makes sense to revisit key concepts multiple times, although this doesn't mean simply repeating everything. You are just as likely to turn your students off out of boredom as help them learn it better if you do this. But you should give them opportunities to experience concepts in a variety of ways. This allows students to make connections between new concepts and similar prior experiences, and to integrate them into their existing knowledge networks.

But again, reviewing and revisiting concepts takes time, so a balance must be struck between the time you need to assess and respond to misconceptions and the pressure you will feel to move on and ensure all the curriculum is covered. It might therefore be worth covering fewer things in depth, and ensuring students really understand these, rather than rushing through everything, but with only limited or shallow understanding. You can identify the key concepts in a particular topic that underpin the most important ideas and prioritise these.

Revisiting concepts with students might also support them by preventing them becoming overloaded as they learn new concepts. Given time and space to reflect on ideas, your students might understand and retain them better.

> ## KEY QUESTIONS
>
> - Read this blog post for some further ideas about the psychology behind helping students' thinking to change: **www.learningscientists.org/blog/2017/7/25-1**
> - Identify the key concepts in an upcoming topic that you will prioritise for reviewing regularly.

CONCLUSION

There are very few things that your students will encounter in school where they will bring absolutely no prior knowledge or connection with them. So, find out about the common misconceptions for an upcoming topic and plan explanations that take these into account, and use a variety of examples and analogies to help you explain ideas. Use assessment at the start of a topic to find out what students already know and monitor how they are developing. Assessment can take many forms, but it should be planned with lesson objectives in mind and used to inform your next steps.

Diagnostic questions are a particularly focused form of assessment that are designed to detect students' underlying misconceptions and help you find out what they think. They work best when they home in on a single idea and are quick to complete.

There is a balance to be struck between covering everything and spending longer on key concepts, which take time to master and should be revisited to ensure they are understood and retained.

KEY CONCEPTS AND FURTHER READING

ANTICIPATING AND RESPONDING TO MISCONCEPTIONS

Allison, S. and Tharby, A. (2015) *Making Every Lesson Count*. Carmarthen: Crown House.

- This book includes practical, evidence-based strategies for effective teaching and learning, including how to address misconceptions.

Fletcher-Wood, H. (2018) *Responsive Teaching.* London: Routledge.

- Based on research into formative assessment and cognitive science, this book offers suggestions to help you support and challenge your students.

ASSESSMENT AND QUESTIONING

Barton, C. (2017) *What Is a Diagnostic Question?* Available at: https://medium.com/eedi/what-is-a-diagnostic-question-13bb85c64062

- This post explains diagnostic questions – what they are and how they can be used.

Moore, A. (n.d.) *Best Evidence Science Teaching: Approaches Diagnostic Questions.* Available at: www.stem.org.uk/sites/default/files/pages/downloads/BEST_Approaches_Diagnostic%20questions.pdf

- This article outlines different types of assessment and includes an appendix of useful formats for diagnostic questions.

National STEM Learning Centre (2017) *The Importance of the Right Questions in Teaching.* Available at: https://about.futurelearn.com/blog/importance-right-questions-teaching

- This post discusses the role of questions to gauge understanding in the classroom.

THRESHOLD CONCEPTS

Kaiser, N. (2018) Threshold concepts and cognition in science: #CogSciSci. *Impact*, 2: 21–2.

- This article further discusses how threshold concepts can be identified, and how you can help students to understand them.

REFERENCES

Department for Education (DfE) (2019) *Early Career Framework.* London: DfE.

McCrea, P. (2019) *Learning: What Is It, and How Might We Catalyse It?* Available at: www.ambition.org.uk/research-and-insight/learning-what-is-it/

Nuthall, G. (2007) *The Hidden Lives of Learners.* Wellington: NZCER Press.

Shtulman, A. and Valcarcel, J. (2012) Scientific knowledge suppresses but does not supplant earlier intuitions. *Cognition*, 124(2): 209–15.

Wiliam, D. (2011) *Embedded Formative Assessment.* Bloomington, IN: Solution Tree Press.

Willingham, D.T. (2004) The privileged status of story. *American Educator*, 28(2): 43–5, 51–3.

14

MARKING AND FEEDBACK

VELDA ELLIOTT

ASSOCIATE PROFESSOR OF ENGLISH AND LITERACY EDUCATION, DIRECTOR OF DOCTORAL RESEARCH, UNIVERSITY OF OXFORD, UK

INTRODUCTION

Feedback is one of the most powerful tools in the teacher's kit in terms of improving learning (Hattie, 2009). It is an almost constant presence in the classroom as it consists of any information you provide to students about their work and how to improve it. Outside the classroom, written marking is one of the most time-consuming parts of teaching. It has the potential to have an impact on student learning, but that time can also be wasted if it is not implemented effectively. Considering what we know about feedback and marking enables you to make sensible decisions about prioritising your time and effort to maximise impact on pupil progress, which is why it features in the Early Career Framework (ECF).

This chapter will summarise what we know about feedback and written marking, and consider why and how it is sometimes difficult for students to act on feedback. It will discuss the challenges and advantages of setting up peer and self-assessment and look at other alternatives to written marking. The most obvious link is to ECF section 6, 'Make Accurate and Productive Use of Assessment', but it also strongly relates to section 5, 'Adaptive Teaching', and section 2, 'Promote Good Progress'.

CHAPTER OBJECTIVES

In this chapter, you will:

- learn about the key characteristics of effective feedback;
- discover barriers to students using feedback to improve;
- consider alternatives to written marking, including spoken feedback;
- think about key ways to make peer and self-assessment effective.

THE IMPORTANCE OF EFFECTIVE FEEDBACK

Feedback is the mechanism by which students learn what level they are working at, the gap between that and the 'desired performance' (i.e. the next stage), and how to bridge that gap (Hattie and Timperley, 2007). This makes it an essential part of classroom practice. Meta-analyses of the effect of feedback suggest that it has a large effect size (e.g. Hattie, 2009), and this is particularly true for primary children and for spoken feedback.

One of the major characteristics that is identified as making feedback effective is that it should be specific. Generic praise or advice (e.g. 'good work', 'explain more') is not usually effective or helpful in improving pupil performance. Specific feedback relates to the task (e.g. exactly what was good, exactly what can be done to improve). It can be operationalised in the form of a target for next time; short-term (e.g. next lesson, not next month), fine-grained targets that are limited in number are shown to work best. In many subjects, the most useful thing to do with targets may be to get students to transcribe the target from their last piece of work at the top of the page when starting a new piece of work, in order to get them to remember it. The need for targets to be short-term means that reminding students of their overall target grades at the end of the year is probably not an effective use of feedback.

The focus of feedback can be on the task, on the person, or on the process of the work (known as self-regulation). Person-focused feedback is usually not effective in improving work (for work on fixed and variable mindset, see also Dweck, 2017). Task-focused feedback is effective, particularly when it is specific, and gets to the nitty-gritty of what a student has got wrong, what is working well, or what can be improved. Finally, thinking about the process can also help students to develop better self-regulation, so feedback that focuses on this aspect – or asks students to reflect on it (e.g. 'How did you make this plan?' 'Where can you go for a hint?') – can also be effective in promoting long-term progress and independent learning.

Timing is important to consider in terms of effective feedback. The most important thing about feedback is that the student should be able to use it to improve going forward. This means, for example, that in subjects such as maths and science, the end-of-unit test may not be the best time to set targets for improvement, because the change of topic often makes those targets irrelevant. On the other hand, it is an ideal time to correct misconceptions and errors in order to prevent them becoming embedded in the students' minds.

Research makes a distinction between mistakes and errors, and suggests treating them in different ways (Elliott et al., 2016). A mistake is an instance where a student knows the underlying pattern or answer but has made a slip. This might be, for instance, omitting one capital letter in a piece of work, or making an arithmetical mistake, or a factual error. Simply identifying that a mistake exists should enable the student to correct it. An error is where there is an underlying pattern indicating the student is lacking a particular item of knowledge or understanding. Errors are often 'treatable' (i.e. if you give students the rule or a hint, they can correct them themselves). Or they may not be treatable, and the student may simply lack the knowledge, in which case giving them the right answer so they can learn it is the right thing to do. Low-level factual questions need rapid correction when students get them wrong as it is easy for them to 'learn' the wrong answer they have given instead of the real one. This means feedback during or immediately after the task in which the error is made.

It is fairly obvious that unless students pay attention to feedback and do something with it, then its effect is likely to be small. It is equally true that written marking, one of the main ways of giving feedback to students (as explored in the next section) is very time-consuming, and spending time on feedback that students then ignore or do not implement is a waste of your time. Therefore, one of the key ways of making feedback effective is to get students to engage with it. Directed/dedicated improvement/independent reflection time (DIRT) is a popular approach – setting aside time at the beginning of a lesson for students to read and act on their feedback. In order to make this effective, a specific exercise or activity is needed, but it is not always appropriate. Doing DIRT for the sake of it can lead to superficial tasks and engagement that do not benefit you or your students. Poor DIRT tasks include asking students to respond to comments rather than doing something specific. Students may also feel that feedback given after the end of a task is less relevant than feedback given mid-task, so be less likely to act on it.

KEY QUESTIONS

- In your subject or age range, what are examples of mistakes versus errors? Do you treat them differently when you see them in student work?

- Are your students paying attention to your feedback? How do you know?

FEEDBACK VIA WRITTEN MARKING

Written marking is by no means the only way of supplying feedback to students, but it is one of the major ways in which we currently do. There are some specific issues to explore in this context. For example, when conducting thorough written marking, beware of the 'proofreading trap' (Cogie et al., 1999). This is when the marker focuses on the easy-to-spot spelling, punctuation and grammar errors, and as a result more fundamental subject discipline issues go unidentified. There is no specific research as to how much feedback information a student can take in at a time, but it is likely that too much will overwhelm them. Focusing on the key thing they need to improve is therefore more likely to be effective.

Another question is how quickly written feedback should be returned to students. It is generally agreed that too long a gap will mean students no longer remember the original task, but how long is too long is an unanswered question. It is likely to vary with age; many primary teachers prefer same- or next-day feedback to prevent students forgetting. In secondary schools, sometimes up to two weeks is given. Part of the problem is the need to balance giving teachers a reasonable time to mark and getting feedback returned in a useful time period.

One major question is that of whether or not to include grades on work. There is a common consensus that the most useful part of written marking in terms of feedback is the comment (Elliott et al., 2016). Grades or marks can distract from that written comment by focusing attention on the summative achievement rather than the feedback and the next steps. However, when students have been used to receiving marks, it takes time to get them used to comment-only marking. In addition, decisions are usually made at the school level as to whether or not grades should be given. You therefore might want to explore the possibility of withholding grades from students until they have read and acted on feedback or completed some feedback task.

KEY QUESTIONS

- Look at some examples of your recent written marking and analyse it for strengths and weaknesses. Was it focused on a particular issue? Are you falling into the 'proofreading trap'?

OVERCOMING BARRIERS TO EFFECTIVE FEEDBACK

Believe it or not, one of the main barriers to feedback being implemented by students is incredibly simple: teacher handwriting. Another barrier can be the words that are used to express the ideas – written feedback is more likely to incorporate formal terms and words from mark schemes, which may not be easily understood. While some students will ask what you have written or what something means, many of them who are most in need of the feedback will not. There is evidence to show that talking to students about their written feedback can be helpful in making sure they understand it (Elliott et al., 2016). This works in several ways: reframing the feedback can help students to understand, initiating a private conversation provides an easier opportunity for them to ask questions, and it fulfils one of the major benefits of feedback and marking – showing that teachers are invested in their students' progress (Blanchard, 2002).

To understand another barrier, think about when you are being observed teaching and receive feedback. Trusting the giver of feedback is essential – both that they have the right expertise and that they have your best interests at heart. This means that a large part of effective feedback comes from developing strong relationships with students in order that they trust, and therefore implement, your feedback. Putting yourself in your students' shoes can also help identify another barrier: the affective aspects of feedback. Receiving feedback can be invested with a lot of emotion. In particular, research has shown that when feedback goes against what the student believes about themselves, particularly if it is critical when they have a generally positive impression of their academic standing, that contrast distracts the student and makes it hard for them to focus (Kluger and DeNisi, 1996). This may mean that feedback has to be couched in certain ways to enable students to adopt it; however, false praise is also identified easily by students and can backfire (Elliott et al., 2016).

KEY QUESTIONS

- Think about a time when you received feedback. How did you feel? What helped or prevented you making use of it? Can you apply this to how you give feedback to your students?

ALTERNATIVES TO WRITTEN MARKING

As many schools are trying to find ways to reduce workload, alternatives to written marking are being increasingly explored. For example, whole-class feedback is becoming popular. There are several varieties of this, but in a typical system the teacher takes in and skims a class set of books (or a few books, representative of the range of attainment in the class, or perhaps focusing on those who had problems during the lesson). They use this skim-read to gain information to adapt their teaching in the next lesson and to provide an activity, or several, to enable students to implement feedback into their work.

Live marking is another popular approach. As teachers circulate the room while students engage in individual or pair work, they spot-check what they are seeing. Identifying mistakes as they happen allows students to correct on the spot and prevents mistakes becoming embedded in their memory. This can also be a very low-stakes way of giving feedback – a simple circle, underline or point in the margin draws the student's attention and gives them a chance to correct themselves if they can, or the opportunity to ask why you have made that mark. It also enables you to stop and reteach something if it is obvious that a large proportion of the class have not grasped the fundamental principle of what they are doing.

Feedback dialogues are another potential way to reduce written marking, although they tend to require an intensive investment of time in the classroom instead. They are more practical in primary environments because of the potential flexibility of the school day and staff deployment. However, feedback dialogues, where you discuss a piece of work with a student rather than marking it in-depth, because they take more time out of the day, also require an acceptance that not everyone will have a dialogue about every piece of work. Instead, everyone in a class will get to talk to the teacher at some point over a given period of time (e.g. every six weeks). Other methods of feedback support this periodic intensive feedback.

Other methods of reducing the time spent marking might include doing some peer or self-marking on classwork, and then you simply look at the problems to identify what the patterns are and adapt future teaching.

For some teachers, the time invested in written marking is a badge of honour – it is something that can be identified as a contribution to pupil progress and is a visible mark of workload. It is important not to get sucked into competitions with others about how long you spent marking in the evening or at the weekend. Many of the alternatives to written marking allow you to spend more time planning good and adaptive teaching (sections 4 and 5), which is a more effective way to use your time. Burnout does not advantage anyone in the long run.

KEY QUESTIONS

- Find out what your school or department feedback policy is and what scope there is for reducing written marking. If there isn't one, what is the norm?

- What are the attitudes to written marking of staff in your school? Who has a healthy approach?

- You may want to try different approaches to find the one that fits you and your class best. After trying one, think about how it worked and whether it was a better investment of your time than marking.

SPOKEN FEEDBACK

Spoken feedback can have a number of advantages over written feedback. Because it happens during class, while students are getting on with their work, there is no gap between the work and the feedback. This also means that feedback comes at the point when it is most likely to be used: mid-task. Since you can see your students' faces while giving them spoken feedback, you can adjust what you are saying accordingly, either to help them understand better or to couch it in ways that makes them more willing to adopt it. It is worth being aware, however, that some children find oral feedback challenging because of the social context of others overhearing what you have to say.

One of the problems with spoken feedback is that students don't always remember what has been said. It can be useful to get them to note down in the margin the key points, which has the added benefit of recording that feedback has been given for parents or school leaders. Depending on your school policy, you may wish to identify when spoken feedback has been given by getting students to correct in another colour or noting 'VF' in the margin. This also helps you to ensure you are distributing your attention around the class equally.

Another approach is to record spoken feedback while looking at finished work instead of writing comments. Various methods can be used for this; one powerful one is to use a tablet computer to film the work and record your comments at the same time. Some teachers like to use websites that generate QR codes for students to scan to access audio feedback. The advantage of this is that audio feedback can be quicker to record than lengthy written notes, and students can replay it or share it with parents. However, there is no clear evidence that this kind of audio recording is more effective than written marking.

KEY QUESTIONS

- Is spoken feedback part of your school feedback policy? Does your senior leadership team (SLT) monitor whether it is happening?

- Choose a lesson and notice how much spoken feedback you give to individuals, small groups and the whole class. Think about how you tailor this feedback to the audience and consider whether this could be used for written marking as well. If not, why not?

PEER AND SELF-FEEDBACK

It is important to distinguish between peer and self-marking, which are useful aids to reducing marking workloads for simple tasks, and peer and self-assessment, which creates useful feedback and contributes to learning in other ways. Taking part in peer and self-assessment activities has a positive effect on attainment (Hattie, 2009).

The quality of the peer feedback is not what makes the difference, but the process of engaging with thinking about current performance and how to improve it. However, students do get better at providing peer feedback over time (Nicolaidou, 2013). To support this, you may want to provide examples of very good work annotated to explain *why* it is good; this enables students to begin to offer advice on how to improve and also to internalise the standards into their own work. The kind of peer and self-assessment activity makes a difference to the advantage gained. Simply generating criteria or sharing assessment criteria with students is not as powerful as getting them engaged in the process of considering feedback on a task, whether to themselves or to others.

Peer and self-feedback are difficult tasks that require investments of time and energy to train up your class so that they know how to engage effectively. Establish ground rules for what you expect from students participating in peer and self-feedback. There need to be structures that focus attention on the key elements of the task, and which enable students to make both positive and constructively critical comments. The more it becomes the norm in your classroom, the less you will have to worry about friendship groups creating a situation where comments are facile or overly positive. One way to circumvent these issues is to require all feedback to be in the form of questions (e.g. 'Why did you do that?' 'What does this mean?' 'Can you provide an example?') and use these to stimulate dialogue between partners. Some researchers have considered the impact of making peer feedback anonymous and have found that students are more willing to offer feedback in these circumstances. This can work well for oral presentations or practical work, or can be established as a norm for written work with slightly more work.

Responding to peer feedback is not necessarily a requirement for it to be effective; it is the process, not the outcome, that seems to be important.

KEY QUESTIONS

- What are the barriers to effective peer and self-assessment in your classroom?
- How long did you spend on setting up peer assessment the last time you used it?

CONCLUSION

The key thing to ask yourself about marking and feedback is whether this particular thing is the most effective use of your time. We have to make decisions about what is sustainable and what is effective, and where the balance comes. Effective feedback is specific, it is task-focused or it helps to improve self-regulation, it is given in a timely fashion, and it does not overwhelm the student. But for feedback to be effective, the most important point is that the student must engage with it – giving it is not enough. Different strategies help students to engage with feedback, including specific tasks, dialogue, live marking, and giving feedback mid-task. One of the most effective ways to give feedback is to adapt your teaching as a result of looking at student work, even though it may feel like it is 'not' feedback. While written marking is often considered to be the main method of delivering feedback, there are alternatives to deep written marking, and oral feedback can be much more powerful. Peer and self-feedback are also key to promoting pupil progress, but they require an investment of time into setting up structures and norms to make them productive. Feedback is a deeply personal thing that relies strongly on relationships between students and teachers, and different students may need different approaches to help them engage best. Finally, remember that sometimes it is important to celebrate work and achievement and pause the seemingly never-ending cycle of next steps to improve.

KEY CONCEPTS AND FURTHER READING

The classic text on feedback is Hattie and Timperley's (2007) review, which provides a model for feedback, and in particular has a section on self-regulation. It is quite dense, however, so is only recommended for those who really want to get into feedback.

A more practical guide, with one chapter that particularly supports peer assessment, is the second edition of *Embedded Formative Assessment* (Wiliam, 2017), which draws on research to create an accessible 'how-to' guide for teachers.

A Marked Improvement? (Elliott et al., 2016) is an accessible brief review on the evidence on written marking published by the Education Endowment Foundation. It summarises what we know (and what we don't!).

━━ REFERENCES ━━

Blanchard, J. (2002) *Teaching and Targets: Self-Evaluation and School Improvement.* London: RoutledgeFalmer.

Cogie, J., Strain, K. and Lorinskas, S. (1999) Avoiding the proofreading trap: the value of the error correction process. *The Writing Center Journal*, 19(2): 7–32.

Dweck, C. (2017) *Mindset – Updated Edition: Changing the Way You Think to Fulfil Your Potential.* London: Robinson.

Elliott, V., Baird, J.A., Hopfenbeck, T.N., Ingram, J., Thompson, I., Usher, N., et al. (2016) *A Marked Improvement? A Review of the Evidence on Written Marking.* London: EEF.

Hattie, J. (2009) *Visible Learning for Teachers: Maximizing Impact on Learning.* London: Routledge.

Hattie, J. and Timperley, H. (2007) The power of feedback. *Review of Educational Research*, 77(1): 81–112.

Kluger, A.N. and DeNisi, A. (1996) The effects of feedback interventions on performance: a historical review, a meta-analysis, and a preliminary feedback intervention theory. *Psychological Bulletin*, 19(2): 254–84.

Nicolaidou, I. (2013) E-portfolios supporting primary students' writing performance and peer feedback. *Computers & Education*, 68: 404–15.

Wiliam, D. (2017) *Embedded Formative Assessment*, 2nd edn. Bloomington, IN: Solution Tree Press.

15

UNDERSTANDING CURRICULUM

MARK PRIESTLEY

PROFESSOR OF EDUCATION, UNIVERSITY OF STIRLING, UK

NIENKE NIEVEEN

ASSOCIATE PROFESSOR AND DIRECTOR OF TEACHER EDUCATION PROGRAMS, UNIVERSITY OF TWENTE, THE NETHERLANDS

INTRODUCTION

Discussion that specifically relates to the school curriculum is firmly back on the educational agenda in the UK after a hiatus of around 25 years. This development is to be welcomed for at least two reasons. First, 'the curriculum is – or at least should be – at the heart of educational discourse and practice' (Priestley and Philippou, 2018, p2). In recent years, there has been a tendency to neglect consideration of curricular issues when developing practice, as schools have become more likely to be influenced by more instrumental concerns driven by accountability systems. Second, teachers play an important role in curriculum-making; policy intentions set out in official curriculum texts only take us so far, and they still need to be translated into practice. This is an active process requiring teachers to work from first principles to develop their practice, and thus requires a good understanding of curriculum (e.g. Nieveen et al., 2010; Priestley et al., 2015).

CHAPTER OBJECTIVES

This chapter provides an introduction to some core curriculum concepts, addressing the following aims, which align closely to section 3 of the Early Career Framework (ECF):

- to set out a framework for understanding curriculum and its role in the development of educational practice;

(Continued)

(Continued)

- to reflect upon the resources required for developing the curriculum;

- to explore issues related to sequencing and progression;

- to reflect upon the relationship between knowledge and skills in the curriculum;

- to suggest implications for curriculum-making by teachers.

These are, of course, complex issues, and so the chapter identifies further reading where applicable.

THE ROLE OF CURRICULUM

Curriculum has been commonly characterised in the UK as content, most often organised into a range of subjects that are familiar to anyone who has attended school. This can lead to narrow thinking and may limit possibilities for curriculum-making in schools. A narrow focus on the 'what' neglects consideration of other big curriculum questions. These include questions relating to purpose (the 'why' of curriculum) and methodologies, including pedagogy, assessment and provision (the 'how' of curriculum). Some curricula have sought to address this issue by expanding the definition of curriculum. For example, Scotland's Curriculum for Excellence has defined curriculum as 'the totality of all that is planned for children and young people throughout their education' (Scottish Government, 2008, p11). While this is helpful up to a point in broadening our view, it is also problematic as it is not specific about what the totality comprises. A more constructive definition is to view curriculum as 'the multi-layered social practices, including infrastructure, pedagogy and assessment, through which education is structured, enacted and evaluated' (Priestley, 2019, p8). This repositions the concept of curriculum; instead of being a product, produced by an external agency and uncritically 'implemented' or 'delivered' by teachers, *the curriculum in school becomes something that practitioners enact or make in their own contexts*. The chapter will adopt the concept of curriculum-making in its subsequent discussion of the curriculum. There are a number of implications that stem from thinking about curriculum in this way.

First, consideration of purpose is important. It is essential that you engage with 'big ideas' underpinning your practice when curriculum-making. Sense-making is important; if you do not fully understand the purposes and principles, then you are likely to develop practices that are not fit for purpose. When new policy emerges, part of the sense-making should be about understanding *how the new differs from the old*. Consideration of the big ideas in a curriculum policy should take place against the backdrop of broader professional discussions about the purposes of education (see the section on organising the curriculum). Second, thinking about curriculum as social practice requires us to consider what those practices might be. Curriculum-making thus includes consideration of knowledge/content based on curricular purposes, but it also involves deliberation about pedagogy (how we learn also shapes the intellect), how we build in opportunities to assess students, and how we might best organise knowledge. The curricular spider's web metaphor (Thijs and van den Akker, 2009) is helpful in allowing us to see the full range of practices that need to be considered in curriculum-making, with 'they' referring to the students (see Figure 15.1). Many of these elements will be considered in the remainder of the chapter.

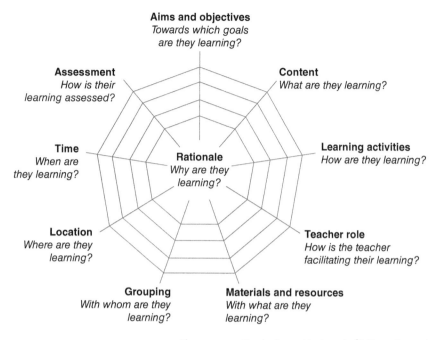

Figure 15.1   Curricular spider's web (Thijs and van den Akker, 2009)

One question relates to whether traditionally configured subjects are the best approach. Subjects have tended to become set in stone, *as ends of education rather than as one means of organising knowledge*, with the hidden risk of gaps, crowding and fragmentation in relation to content. Instead, we could consider whether the appropriate question for planning the curriculum is, 'What knowledge, skills and attributes should a young person develop?' as opposed to the more commonplace, 'What subjects should be taught?' Of course, this question should be grounded in the question of purpose – what schools are for – and guided by a principle of fitness for purpose. In terms of pedagogy, this also requires you to think about *how new knowledge might be acquired*. For example, when is it appropriate to engage in direct instruction (such as for building systematic concept maps), and when are student-centred methods (such as student dialogue and inquiry) more applicable?

SELECTION OF RESOURCES

Curriculum-making is dependent on – and shaped by – the availability of resources. These can be *material, cognitive* or *relational*. Material resources include textbooks and other teaching materials (e.g. downloaded from websites). Selection and use of material resources needs to be planned carefully in order to ensure that pedagogy is supported in a way that aligns with curricular purposes. For example, you may wish to consider what resources are required to support a particular type of activity (e.g. cooperative learning, direct instruction), but you should also consider *what the activity aims to achieve* (e.g. development of deep understanding of a concept already taught directly, initial development of a basic concept map). Material resources also include the physical spaces where learning and teaching take place, including the wider school environment and outdoor spaces. These can either enable or seriously limit curriculum-making.

ORGANISING THE CURRICULUM

Many modern curricula have been criticised for downgrading knowledge, instead over-focusing on skills development. In England, conversely, the curriculum has been criticised for reducing knowledge to the memorisation of facts (for an overview of different approaches, see Young and Muller, 2010). The next section will address the issue of balance between skills and knowledge; here, the authors make the case for the importance of knowledge, while accepting the principle that this needs to be selected by practitioners as part of a coherent approach to developing understanding over time. One of the basic questions that curriculum-makers need to consider carefully is, 'What knowledge is of most worth?' This is not an easy question. What should count as knowledge? What types of knowledge are essential? Answering these types of questions relates to the position you take regarding the purposes of education. One framing is provided by Biesta (2015):

- *Qualification*: Education needs to provide students with the necessary knowledge, skills and dispositions.

- *Socialisation*: Education needs to assist students to become part of and identify with the existing social, cultural and political practices and traditions.

- *Subjectification*: Education needs to help students to become the unique individuals that they can be.

Ideally, a comprehensive curriculum will cover all three purposes in a balanced way. Nevertheless, the design of a curriculum depends on the purpose(s) you prioritise. A curriculum that emphasises qualification tends to be subject-oriented with the following essential concepts: objectives, sequential learning, direct instruction, and achievement testing. A curriculum that focuses mainly on socialisation and/or social reconstruction may focus on meeting the needs of, or developing, society. A curriculum that aims at subjectification is usually individual-centred. For this latter orientation, Klein (1999) suggests that students need to become the curriculum developers, and the curriculum is thus not pre-planned by adults.

Sequencing issues are mainly related to the subject-oriented curriculum. Here, next to the question, 'What knowledge is of most worth?' you also need to make decisions about the way in which the curriculum is best organised. Tyler (1949) wrote, in his famous book *Basic Principles of Curriculum and Instruction*, that organising is an important issue in curriculum development. Changes in students develop slowly: 'by the culmination of educational experiences, profound changes are brought about in the learner. In order for educational experiences to produce a cumulative effect, they must be so organized as to reinforce each other' (p83).

Regarding organising the curriculum, a major foundation has been provided by Bruner, who coined the idea of the spiral curriculum in the 1960s. According to Bruner (1960):

The foundations of any subject may be taught to anybody at any age in some form … A curriculum as it develops should revisit these basic ideas repeatedly, building upon them until the student has grasped the full formal apparatus that goes with them.

(p12)

A spiral curriculum shows the progression of learning. When you design a spiral curriculum, first you have to decide on the big ideas (or key concepts, central questions, major curriculum elements). These are long-term considerations that are significant for the field you are about to teach, and form the organising threads. There are three guiding criteria when further organising the learning experiences of the students, already identified by Tyler and still in use:

- *Continuity*: Refers to the organisation over time. Vertical relations are facilitated when courses are organised over a period of years in larger units and when the key concepts are reiterated.

- *Sequence*: Refers to the importance of successive experiences that build on one another and that go more broadly and deeply into the concepts that are involved. Posner and Rudnitsky (1986) provide an array of broadening and deepening sequencing principles: (1) world-related sequences (e.g. space, time); (2) concept-related sequences (e.g. class relations, propositional relations); (3) inquiry-related sequences (e.g. logic of inquiry); (4) learning-related sequences (e.g. empirical prerequisite, familiarity, difficulty); and (5) utilisation-related sequences (e.g. procedure, anticipated frequency of utilisation).

- *Integration*: Refers to combining the concepts with the broader field in order to help pupils get a more unified view on the matters.

Advantages of creating learning progressions are that they promote the reiteration, deepening, broadening and integration of key concepts, which in turn assist students in strengthening their understanding. Moreover, learning progressions assist teachers and students in tailoring lesson planning to support student learning. Nevertheless, it is important that you make tentative decisions regarding the learning progressions, prevent them from being too fine-grained, and test them to see whether they indeed assist in developing continuity, sequence and integration.

KNOWLEDGE AND SKILLS

A significant issue that has characterised debate around the curriculum in the UK concerns the development of spurious dichotomies. These include knowledge versus skills, children versus subjects, 'sage on the stage' versus 'guide on the side', and 'traditional' versus 'progressive'. The knowledge versus skills debate has become especially pernicious. Advocates of the former decry the instrumental focus of curricula that seek to develop skills, instead calling for curricula based in essential knowledge or 'cultural literacy'. Conversely, advocates of a skills-based curriculum assert that we are preparing children for jobs that do yet not exist, or claim that knowledge is now at everyone's fingertips via Google. These either/or positions are unhelpful. Knowledge and skills are not easily separable. According to Gill and Thomson (2012), 'this dichotomy is a false one because knowing can consist of a complex set of skills' (p37). They suggest that much knowledge is about concept-building, and to possess a concept is the skill of being 'able to recognize relevant similarities and differences' (p37). This is not new thinking; John Dewey (1907), regarded by many as the father of progressive education, explicitly rejected what he saw as the false dichotomy of knowledge and process, emphasising the importance of the accumulated wisdom of the world. According to Hofkins and Northen (2009), 'there is an easy way to eliminate these facile, but dangerous, dichotomies' (p41). This is to 'simply substitute "and" for "not" and "versus"' (p41).

It is perhaps more constructive to view knowledge and skills as different types of knowledge. For instance, one can classify what is generally termed knowledge as *propositional knowledge* – 'knowing that'. This includes facts, first-order concepts that are specific to a subject (e.g. monarchy in history), and second-order generic concepts (e.g. continuity and change). Skills may be better classified as *procedural knowledge* – 'knowing how'. A key challenge in curriculum-making is to identify how these different forms of knowledge interrelate, thus achieving a balance between them.

KEY QUESTIONS

It is worth noting here the central importance of the teacher in developing a coherent curriculum that systematically enables students to build concept maps and deepen understanding. This involves pedagogical questions. For example:

- When is it appropriate to practise a skill in order to gain mastery?

- When is dialogue helpful to deepen understanding?

- When is it best for you to explicitly develop conceptual framings through direct instruction?

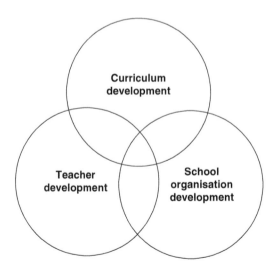

Figure 15.2   Three interrelated developments at the school level

CONCLUSIONS

Sustainable (school-wide) curriculum change needs productive relations between curriculum development, professional development of teachers, and school organisation development (see Figure 15.2).

Regarding curriculum development, the spider's web metaphor in Figure 15.1 illustrates that the components of the envisaged curriculum need to form a coherent set: all components have to be addressed when changing the curriculum. With respect to teacher development, it is important to note that major curriculum changes also imply a need for change in at least three dimensions, as suggested by Fullan (2007): new pedagogies, new materials and altered beliefs. Moreover, teachers need to become collaborative curriculum designers who, for instance, create meaningful connections between knowledge and skills of adjacent subject areas. For the school organisation, this means that it should become a powerful learning, teaching and design environment, fostering a culture of collaboration and accountability and developing structures that are helpful in this kind of school culture. These include suitable workspaces for joint work, opportunities for learning inside and outside school, crossover structures, and regular communication to all staff in the school about progress. Curriculum change that integrates these developments is at the heart of the model introduced in Figure 15.2 (cf. Handelzalts et al., 2019).

Successful curriculum change calls for a layered approach, including efforts at the classroom level, the school level and the system level, such as top-down guidance from the government and lateral support from teacher education, textbooks and other resources, support agencies, and other schools (cf. Nieveen and Plomp, 2017). The takeaway message is that to initiate a curriculum change, it takes efforts and courage from all involved, not just the teachers, to end up with sustainable results.

In summary, when working as a teacher on curriculum matters at the classroom or school level, you need to feel that you have the curriculum capacity to do the job based on your past experiences. You need to be able to envisage the future opportunities regarding the new curriculum. Moreover, the circumstances inside and outside the school should allow you to make the curriculum change happen. If all of these elements are present, your agency as a curriculum-maker will be considerably enhanced (Priestley et al., 2015).

KEY CONCEPTS AND FURTHER READING

DEFINING THE CONCEPT OF CURRICULUM

Marsh, C.J. and Willis, G. (2007) *Curriculum: Alternative Approaches, Ongoing Issues*. Columbus, OH: Pearson/Merrill Prentice Hall.

- This introductory book helps in uncovering and clarifying the complex nature of curriculum. Like in this chapter, the authors start from the notion that the curriculum is better understood as a composite of what is intended for the classroom (planned curriculum), what happens in the classroom (the enacted curriculum), and how what happens influences individuals (the experienced curriculum).

TEACHERS AS CURRICULUM-MAKERS

Skilbeck, M. (1984) *School-Based Curriculum Development*. London: Harper & Row.

- School-based curriculum development and the role of teachers as curriculum-makers is not a new idea in curriculum discussions. For instance, Skilbeck's work contributed in many ways towards a better understanding of school-based curriculum development and how it may be undertaken.

TEACHER AGENCY

Priestley, M., Biesta, G. and Robinson, S. (2015) *Teacher Agency: An Ecological Approach*. London: Bloomsbury Academic.

- This book is an important source on what teacher agency entails from a curricular perspective. It discusses the concept in respect of the cultures and structures of schooling and discusses the implications for the layered educational system.

REFERENCES

Biesta, G. (2015) What is education for? On good education, teacher judgment, and educational professionalism. *European Journal of Education*, 50(1): 75–87.

Bruner, J.S. (1960) *The Process of Education*. Cambridge, MA: Harvard University Press.

Dewey, J. (1907) Waste in education. In J. Dewey (ed.), *The School and Society: Being Three Lectures by John Dewey Supplemented by a Statement of the University Elementary School*. Chicago, IL: University of Chicago Press, pp77–100.

Fullan, M. (2007) *The New Meaning of Educational Change*. New York: Teachers College Press.

Gill, S. and Thomson, G. (2012) *Rethinking Secondary Education: A Human-Centred Approach*. London: Pearson.

Handelzalts, A., Nieveen, N. and van den Akker, J. (2019) Teacher design teams for school-wide curriculum development: reflections on an early study. In J. Pieters, J. Voogt and N. Pareja Roblin (eds), *Collaborative Curriculum Design: Sustainable Curriculum Innovation and Teacher Learning*. Cham: Springer, pp55–82.

Hofkins, D. and Northen, S. (2009) *Introducing the Cambridge Primary Review*. Cambridge: University of Cambridge, Faculty of Education.

Klein, F. (1999) Alternative curriculum conceptions and designs. In A.C. Ornstein and L.S. Behar-Horenstein (eds), *Contemporary Issues in Curriculum*. Boston, MA: Allyn & Bacon, pp30–5.

Nieveen, N. and Plomp, T. (2017) Curricular and implementation challenges in introducing twenty-first century skills in education. In E. Care, P. Griffin and M. Wilson (eds), *Assessment and Teaching of 21st Century Skills*. Cham: Springer, pp59–76.

Nieveen, N., van den Akker, J. and Resink, F. (2010) Framing and supporting school-based curriculum development in the Netherlands. In E.H.-F. Law and N. Nieveen (eds), *Schools as Curriculum Agencies: Asian and European Perspectives on School-Based Curriculum Development*. Rotterdam: Sense Publishers, pp273–83.

Posner, G.J. and Rudnitsky, A.N. (1986) *Course Design: A Guide to Curriculum Development for Teachers*. New York: Longman.

Priestley, M. (2019) Curriculum: concepts and approaches. *Impact*, 6: 5–8.

Priestley, M. and Philippou, S. (2019) Curriculum is – or should be – at the heart of educational practice. *The Curriculum Journal*, 30(1): 1–7.

Priestley, M., Biesta, G. and Robinson, S. (2015) *Teacher Agency: An Ecological Approach.* London: Bloomsbury Academic.

Scottish Government (2008) *Building the Curriculum 3: A Framework for Learning and Teaching.* Edinburgh: Scottish Government.

Thijs, A. and van den Akker, J. (2009) *Curriculum in Development.* Enschede: SLO.

Tyler, R.W. (1949) *Basic Principles of Curriculum and Instruction.* Chicago, IL: University of Chicago Press.

Young, M. and Muller, J. (2010) Three educational scenarios for the future: lessons from the sociology of knowledge. *European Journal of Education*, 45(1): 11–27.

16

PLANNING CURRICULUM AND PROGRESSION

CLARE SEALY

HEAD OF CURRICULUM AND STANDARDS, OFFICE OF THE COMMITTEE FOR EDUCATION, SPORT AND CULTURE, STATES OF GUERNSEY

INTRODUCTION

In this chapter, you will learn about section 3 of the Early Career Framework (ECF) on developing good subject and curriculum knowledge. The framework includes this because while generic teaching skills such as behaviour management and the ability to communicate clearly are important, it is also vital that you fully understand the content you are teaching. If you only have a superficial grasp of your subject area, you run the risk of passing on misconceptions that you yourself might hold. This might seem harsh, but there is substantial research, particularly with regard to the teaching of science, showing that even science teachers with science degrees can hold misconceptions about some scientific concepts (Kikas, 2004). As well as good subject knowledge, if you want to ensure your students really understand what you are teaching them and remember it in the long term, you also need to understand how to sequence concepts so that easier concepts or examples are taught before harder ones. Progress consists in students acquiring a more sophisticated understanding of the full range of a concept over time.

In some schools, the curriculum has already been worked out with careful curriculum progression explicitly in mind. Other schools are at an earlier stage on this journey. Whichever stage your school is at, you will need to understand why the concepts in your curriculum are taught in the order they are and play your part within your staff team in reflecting upon whether or not this is the most appropriate way of sequencing learning.

THE TROUBLE WITH MEASURING PROGRESS

Until recently, schools thought about progress in terms of numerical values – points of progress – with teachers tasked with ensuring their students made a certain number of points per term. This idea is on the wane for

CHAPTER OBJECTIVES

In this chapter, you will learn:

- to understand what it means to make progress in learning;

- to understand the curriculum has a structure that enables progress over time;

- to understand the role of schemata in enabling students to build increasingly complex mental models;

- to reflect on the role that examples and non-examples play in developing understanding.

a number of reasons, of which two will be outlined here. First, when viewed over the course of years rather than months, it is clear that students make progress in fits and starts, with plateaus, rises and indeed falls, rather than following a smooth linear trajectory (Treadaway, 2015). Second, and more seriously, averaging out attainment within a subject to a single numerical value obscures more than it illuminates. Averages, by their very nature, smooth out peaks and troughs in performance. What if the trough involves a really fundamental part of the subject, without which the student will find it difficult to make progress further down the line? If a student deploys varying compensating strategies that enable them to appear – at least on a spreadsheet – to be performing adequately, critical areas they have not yet learnt may remain. These compensating strategies will only take them so far. At some point in the future, probably when they are now the responsibility of some other teacher, this gap may become a sinkhole. Further progress will slow or stall because the necessary foundations are not securely in place.

For example, if a child learns to guess at the meaning of words using picture and meaning cues rather than being able to decode words using phonics, it might seem like they are learning to read well. However, as soon as they encounter harder texts with few pictures and trickier syntax, they flounder. Similarly, students who have got by in maths by being extremely fast at counting but who have never committed any number bonds to heart might initially appear to be coping well, but then falter when faced with more complicated maths which assumes that the student already knows what the sum of six and eight is without having to resort to counting.

This second problem with numerical systems is highly problematic. By incentivising teachers to average out pupil performance into some single numerical grade, level or score to 'prove' that their students have made progress, teaching is frequently distorted away from what the student really needs to learn in order to make genuine long-term progress and towards what will deliver the next numerical benchmark. Tragically, the quest to measure progress has impeded the kind of teaching that enables actual progress.

Given these shortcomings, many schools are looking for better ways of understanding progress. Crucially, such a new system must help, not hinder, the teacher in identifying and then teaching what students need to learn at that moment – in other words, assessment that serves the curriculum rather than a curriculum that serves the assessment system.

KEY QUESTIONS

- To what extent do you feel under pressure to 'prove' progress, even at the expense of teaching the things that will underpin genuine progress?

- How well do you know if the students you teach really have the basics from previous year groups secure?

- If they don't, what could you do to make sure these gaps are addressed?

THE CURRICULUM AS THE PROGRESSION MODEL

If we stop thinking about progress in terms of numbers, what does making progress really mean? If you want to know if your students are making progress, you will need to know what kind of tangible achievements you are looking for. What do your students now know that they didn't know before? What can they now do that they couldn't do before? How appropriate are the decisions your students make about choosing to take one course of action rather than another? Do they remember what you and your colleagues have taught them not only at the end of a topic, but months or years later? Can they use what they have learnt in one context and apply that flexibly in another?

It is the answers to these questions that will tell you whether or not your students are making progress. Students make progress by deepening or widening understanding just as much as by moving on to work of greater difficulty. In order to ask and answer these questions, you will need to know what it is you want your students to know and to do. You will also need to understand how knowing or being able to do a particular thing lays the foundation for being able to do something else later. In other words, you will need to understand how the curriculum you are teaching structures progress over time by gradually introducing new material in a carefully sequenced way where previous learning paves the way for later learning.

This is more obvious in subjects where the curriculum is hierarchical, such as most of maths. For example, before learning how to add fractions with different denominators, students will need to already understand what it is to add, that a denominator is an operator rather than a quantity, why this means you can't just add denominators, how different fractions can be of equivalent value, how to find a common denominator by using times table facts, and so on. There are essential prerequisites that need to be in place. If your students do not understand that denominators are operators rather than quantities, in the short term they might remember that they need to find an equivalent fraction prior to adding. They might score well in an end-of-unit test. However, if this building block is missing, when faced with adding fractions some time later, much to your consternation, they may well revert to adding the two denominators together. What is more, years later they may become utterly confused when learning to manipulate algebraic fractions. Within hierarchical subjects, there is an obvious sequence of steps that your planning needs to anticipate both in terms of what you yourself will teach but also in terms of laying the foundations for what will come later, maybe several years later. Our accountability system may give you no credit for preparing the ground for what is to come at some future date, but the moral purpose that animates your teaching will drive you to do this because it is the right thing to do.

Other subjects do not have the same sort of hierarchical structure. History, for example, is cumulative rather than hierarchical. While there are arguments for learning history chronologically, it does not really matter whether you learn about the Romans before you learn about the Second World War, or vice versa. But that is not to say that there is no need for coherence within a history curriculum. Imagine a student is learning about the Roman invasion of Britain. When we learn, we make sense of new material by building upon what we already know. In this case, you would want students to already know what a soldier was and where Britain is prior to introducing them to the concept of invasion. Imagine a couple of years later these same students learn about the Second World War. Because these students have already studied the Roman invasion of Britain, they already understand not only the concept of invasion, but also various associated concepts, such as resistance, and the factors that enable or thwart invasion, such as infrastructure and technology. Imagine these same students, now in secondary school learning about the First World War, drawing on their previous learning when understanding the logistical challenges of trench warfare.

Coherent curriculum design involves thinking about the learning journey over time and how what is learnt at one point lays the foundation for later learning, maybe many years later. For example, think about a Year 10 geography student studying soil erosion. The foundations for understanding these concepts started ten years ago when in reception class they gained first-hand experience of sand and mud in the sandpit and mud kitchen. Over the intervening years, learning about root structure, soil composition and permeability, soil particle size, factors affecting soil fertility, the effects of volcanic eruptions on soil composition, grazing habits of different animals, factors that accelerate evaporation, differences between nomadic and settled forms of life, patterns of agriculture, and understanding the carbon cycle all contribute to how well a student is able to understand the concept of soil erosion and think critically about ways in which it could be mitigated. Students do not start learning these concepts from scratch in Year 10. Their understanding is built upon layers of previous learning, stretching back throughout their school career.

KEY QUESTIONS

- Think about a topic you are soon to teach. What do you think are the essential prerequisites a student needs to have before they will be able to understand what you are about to teach them?
- Which subjects do you think are mainly hierarchical and which mainly cumulative?

SCHEMATA: BUILDING COMPLEX MENTAL MODELS

Students make progress as the mental models they have become more complex, more sophisticated, enabling them to think and act in more complex and sophisticated ways. These mental models are known as schemata, webs of interrelated concepts linked together and stored in our long-term memories (Didau, 2018). For example, if you think about the word 'car', you will probably implicitly know that a car is a form of transport, has four wheels, is usually powered by petrol, drives on roads, and so on. Each person's schemata are individual. The links made that join concepts together vary from person to person, although with significant overlap. When you think about the word 'car', you will probably have made slightly different links to your neighbour.

You may be a keen follower of Formula One, whereas she may not drive at all and think that cars are an ecological disaster. You may have an extensive database of different types of car and their relative merits, whereas she might lump all cars together as just cars but have a similarly developed understanding of different types of pushbikes.

Curriculum planning involves thinking about the kinds of links we want to encourage students to develop. When a student first encounters something, their understanding of it will be limited because it will not be linked to very much else. Good curriculum design will expose students to carefully selected examples that enable them to make links with other related aspects of whatever is under study, and over time develop a much more sophisticated way of thinking about it. Take, for example, how a young child might think about the word 'animal'. They might have a rather limited schema and think of animals solely in terms of four-legged furry things. They might struggle when told that a duck or a human is an animal, because the lack of fur, or four legs, violates the way they have organised their schema. A well-thought-out science curriculum will take this on board and deliberately set out to challenge such misconceptions. Over time, the curriculum will introduce students to an ever-more diverse series of examples, allowing the student to develop increasingly sophisticated ways of thinking about a concept.

Consider the concept of agriculture. A child might begin to learn about agriculture at school in the early years when singing 'Old MacDonald Had a Farm', hearing stories set on farms, visiting a farm, and playing with toy farm animals. This is then built upon in Key Stage 1 when they learn about the harvest and that some farms do not have any animals at all. At the same time, the child's understanding of flowering plants is expanded by encountering wheat and barley and by learning about what plants need to live. In lower Key Stage 2, they learn about the Stone Age and the beginnings of farming, then later about rainforests and how not all crops are edible. In upper Key Stage 2, the child learns to compare and contrast urban and rural settlements and consider different patterns of land use. In Key Stage 3, a basic understanding of farming is taken as read within the history curriculum when studying the life of peasants in medieval England. Meanwhile, in geography, sustainable farming practices are being studied via a variety of different case studies. Thus, by the time the student enters Year 10 and learns about soil erosion, they have a sophisticated mental model with which to consider the subject matter. It is not that the curriculum has been constructed purely with the aim of enabling the student to think critically about soil erosion, but that by helping students develop complex thinking structures comprised of well-connected, well-organised knowledge, we equip them to be able to think about a wide range of things.

KEY QUESTIONS

- Think about the concept of energy or monarchy. What is in your schema for energy? Compare your schema with that of a colleague. What do you think the schema of a child in your class might look like?

THE ROLE OF EXAMPLES AND NON-EXAMPLES

When students are at the very beginnings of learning about something, the examples you choose should be the most typical, straightforward and obvious. So, for example, if you are teaching children about birds, you should start with the most typical kinds of birds that exemplify the most typical characteristics: wings, feathers, beaks, and so on. But later on, the curriculum should introduce them to less typical birds (e.g. flightless birds, birds that break some of the rules generally used to categorise birds). Think about the examples that lie on the boundary and, crucially, expose students to non-examples, examples of things that appear to share some of the features of typical birds and yet are not birds (Bunsen Blue, 2019). Why is it, for example, that a moth or a bat is not a bird yet a penguin is? How like a bird is it possible to be and yet not be a bird? When students can answer these types of questions, you will know that they now have a deeper understanding of the concept you wish them to learn.

When teaching about triangles, for example, it is usual to start with the prototypical equilateral triangle oriented with the base downwards. Over a series of lessons, an ever-more diverse selection of triangles (e.g. isosceles, right-angled, scalene) will be shared with students. The teacher will take pains to make sure that these different triangles are shown to children in a variety of orientations, not just base downwards. The teacher will make sure that they include examples that exemplify the boundary conditions by including examples that look like they might be triangles but aren't (e.g. three-sided figures with curved sides, three-sided figures where two or more of the lines don't meet).

Sometimes this exposure to a range of examples takes place within one lesson or within a series of related lessons. Sometimes it is sufficient to only cover the simplest examples of something because learning about more nuanced or complicated examples will be covered in later years, and to include the full diversity of examples too early would be likely to confuse. For example, when teaching young children about Islam, learning about the Five Pillars is a sensible starting place. However, while the Five Pillars are foundational for Sunni Muslims, Shia Muslims and Ismaili Muslims describe their faith in slightly different ways. But it would be overcomplicated to teach children about this diversity of belief too early. When teaching children about gravity, at first it is appropriate to talk in a simplified way about gravity making things fall down. You will be aware, though, that this is a simplification, and that at some future point this simplification will be countered with a more complicated explanation about gravity being a force of attraction between two objects: it is not only the case that a person is attracted to the centre of the Earth; the Earth is also attracted to the centre of the person.

Good curriculum design explicitly pinpoints common misconceptions students have and deliberately addresses these not once, but many times. A misconception occurs when knowledge is connected together incorrectly, when the wrong links are made with a schema. For example, since with natural numbers the value of a number increases by one from one number in the counting sequence to another, it is entirely understandable that students will think that denominators, which are rational numbers rather than natural numbers, will increase in value in the same way. They will link (incorrectly) their prior understanding of the value of natural numbers with their understanding of the value of denominators, and therefore conclude that the higher the denominator, the higher the value. The maths curriculum must address this misconception head-on. To give another example, in geography, children frequently have the misconception that all deserts are hot and sandy, whereas the correct definition of a desert is that it is very dry. Curriculum design in geography will need to explicitly include examples of cold, dry deserts such as Antarctica in order to address this misconception.

When addressing misconceptions, bear in mind that when we learn something that conflicts with what we previously thought to be true, it seems that the misconception is only suppressed, not entirely supplanted. In other words, the misconception lingers on within our schema and can occasionally resurface, even though another part of us no longer believes it to be true. The incorrect link still exists, though alongside it there is now also the correct link. In order to ensure that the 'old' link does not reassert itself, you need to make sure that the 'new' link is much stronger. This is why just explaining to students once or twice why something is not correct is often not successful. The misconception is often grounded in folk wisdom or everyday experience, so will have been reinforced many times, making the link very strong. In order to overcome the misconception, you need to make the new link even stronger, and this will involve repeated practice. Imagine the two links as two roads. The student is used to travelling down the old road. You will need to ensure your students drive again and again down the new road. Over time, with repeated use, the new road becomes a superhighway, while the old road, fallen into disuse, becomes but a dirt track.

KEY QUESTIONS

- What are the most likely misconceptions students may form? What can you do to help them overcome these misconceptions?

- Think about a range of examples you might use to explain a concept. Which examples are more prototypical, and which lie nearer to the boundary? Can you think of some non-examples that will help reduce misconceptions?

CONCLUSION

The acquisition of more information is not, by itself, sufficient for a student to make progress. Students make progress not just by learning more 'stuff' as if hoarding more and more facts was the hallmark of a well-educated person, but by being guided to develop increasingly sophisticated ways of thinking and acting. This cultivation of more complex schemata is what it means to make progress and the fundamental principle underlying good curriculum design.

KEY QUESTIONS

- 'If students have gaps in their learning from several years ago, it is the duty of the teacher to address these gaps, even if this means not covering all of the material within the curriculum for the present year group.' Discuss whether you agree or disagree, and what the advantages and disadvantages of so doing might be.

- 'Teachers should have the autonomy to choose what they want to teach, based on their own interests and those of their children.' How far is this point of view compatible with coherent curriculum progression? Which is more important, teacher autonomy or curriculum coherence? Why?

KEY CONCEPTS AND FURTHER READING

- Using numbers to try to measure progress, especially when used in an accountability framework, can distort what is taught to the detriment of genuine progress. See:

Christodoulou, D. (2016) *Making Good Progress*. Oxford: Oxford University Press.

- Progress should be structured into a curriculum as students learn to think and act in more complex and sophisticated ways over time. See:

Myatt, M. (2018) *The Curriculum: Gallimaufry to Coherence*. Woodbridge: John Catt Education.

- Schemata are mental models used for thinking and acting. See:

Didau, D. (2018) *How to Explain ... Schema*. Available at: https://learningspy.co.uk/featured/how-to-explain-schema/

- Examples and non-examples play a crucial role in exemplifying the boundary conditions of a concept. See:

Bunsen Blue (2019) *Clear Teacher Explanations I: Examples and Non-Examples*. Available at: https://bunsenblue.wordpress.com/2019/10/20/clear-teacher-explanations-i-examples-non-examples/

- Misconceptions are formed when concepts are linked together incorrectly within schemata. See:

American Psychological Association (2019) *How Do I Get My Students over Their Alternative Conceptions (Misconceptions) for Learning?* Available at: www.apa.org/education/k12/misconceptions

REFERENCES

Bunsen Blue (2019) *Clear Teacher Explanations I: Examples and Non-Examples*. Available at https://bunsenblue.wordpress.com/2019/10/20/clear-teacher-explanations-i-examples-non-examples/

Didau, D. (2018) *How to Explain ... Schema*. Available at: https://learningspy.co.uk/featured/how-to-explain-schema/

Kikas, E. (2004) *Teachers' Conceptions and Misconceptions concerning Three Natural Phenomena*. Available at: https://onlinelibrary.wiley.com/doi/abs/10.1002/tea.20012

Treadaway (2015) *Why Measuring Pupil Progress Involves More Than Taking a Straight Line*. Available at: https://ffteducationdatalab.org.uk/2015/03/why-measuring-pupil-progress-involves-more-than-taking-a-straight-line/

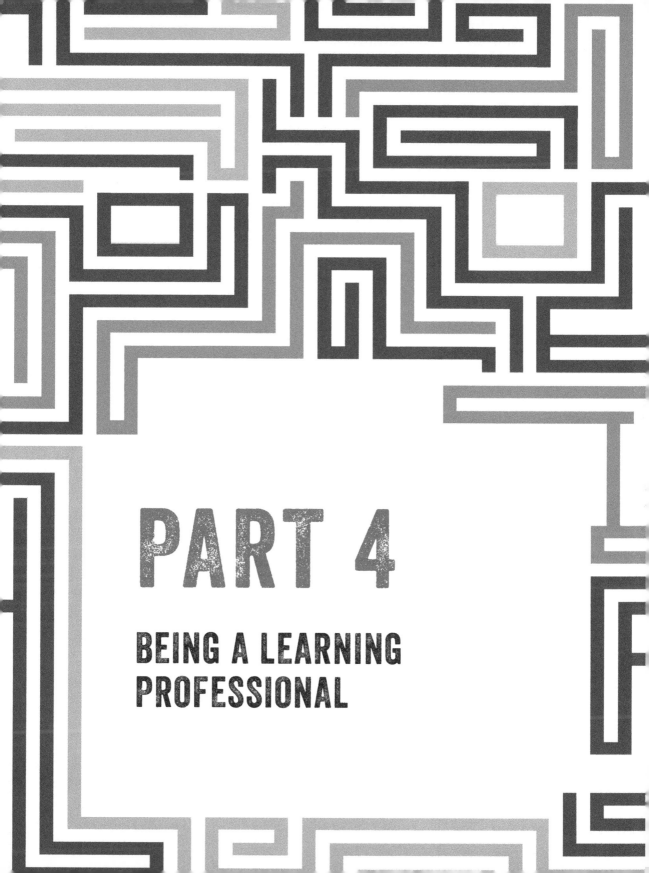

PART 4

BEING A LEARNING PROFESSIONAL

17

PROFESSIONAL LEARNING AND GROWTH

REUBEN MOORE

EXECUTIVE DIRECTOR, TEACH FIRST, UK

FAYE CRASTER

DIRECTOR OF TEACHER DEVELOPMENT, TEACH FIRST, UK

INTRODUCTION

Research has shown that the thing that has the biggest impact on pupil outcomes is the quality of teaching. The best way to improve the quality of teaching is high-quality and rigorous development and support of teachers. In this chapter, we will explore why professional development is important, and how you can get the most out of the opportunities you have to grow and develop.

> ### CHAPTER OBJECTIVES
>
> In this chapter, you will learn:
>
> - why teachers need to develop;
> - how to make the most out of mentoring and coaching;
> - how to prepare for and get the most from conferences or workshops;
> - how to reflect on your practice to help you improve;
> - how you can benefit from networks;
> - how to practise.

WHY DO TEACHERS NEED TO DEVELOP?

It might seem obvious for those working as teachers that the demands of the job require a continuous approach to development. Even experienced teachers are constantly needing to develop in response to curriculum changes, new policies, pupil needs, additional responsibilities, new research, technology changes, and a whole host of other reasons. As an early career teacher, you will no doubt have experienced a huge growth in your own practice from your very early days on your initial teacher training (ITT) course. But we know that teaching is incredibly complex; it's hard to be a great teacher every day alongside constantly expanding your knowledge and skills. It's therefore integral for all teachers that professional learning opportunities are of the highest quality and make the best use of your time. Also, getting better at things builds motivation. Dan Pink (2009) talks about the importance of jobs having purpose, autonomy and mastery; teaching is a great profession where these three elements are present.

When teaching PGCE sessions, Christine Counsell used to describe history lessons as fairy cake or fruit cake. The first tastes great and is enjoyable to eat, but will leave you unsatisfied and hungry once the sugar rush has gone. However, fruit cake is more substantial and probably marginally better for you, and may leave you less hungry. It may be enjoyable at the time, but fairy cake professional development will leave you unsatisfied, and you may not even remember it once you get to the car park, never mind have the ability to implement the actions from it. Good professional development therefore has to be more 'fruit cake' – it needs to be more sustaining.

WHAT IS GOOD PROFESSIONAL DEVELOPMENT?

There are numerous definitions, but in order to be considered effective we believe that good professional development:

- is grounded in research;

- has a clear focus;

- will help teachers improve pupil outcomes;

- includes collaboration and challenge;

- is delivered by experts;

- fits into a sequence of learning;

- can be implemented in practice;

- is prioritised by school leaders.

Alongside this list of criteria of what makes it good, professional development can be done in a variety of ways, which can mostly be categorised into a range of different components. It is unlikely that effective professional development will be reduced to one of these components. Instead, most programmes will utilise all of them.

Coaching

Often this is used when people have developed expertise. They don't need further specific instruction, but instead perhaps need time, space and someone to push them to think about how they will solve problems they are facing.

Academic writing

The process of writing can be hugely beneficial to practice. It is usually within formal programmes at universities. It gives you the opportunity to explore research, understand, critique, test some of the ideas and then share results, and leads to further questions for enquiry.

Mentoring

This is where an expert provides guidance and advice to move someone forward.

Online courses

Online learning can have huge benefits, not least because it can often be accessed at a time that works for you.

Deliberate practice

The opportunity to rehearse with an expert can be hugely beneficial for teacher development. It is, however, hard to do well.

Independent reflection

Using different models of reflection to learn from your own practice can help create bespoke development objectives and also help you recognise successes in your teaching.

Workshops/conferences

As standalone events, individual workshops or conferences are often criticised for not creating sustained change in practice, but they can be hugely valuable in gaining insight from expert colleagues across the sector. Either way, what is important is to reflect on what you have learnt.

Collaborative working (e.g. co-planning)

Working alongside a peer, particularly someone who is more expert in the area, can be incredibly developmental. Similarly, networks can be a great source of advice, resources and support.

Self-Study

This will mostly be reading and is great for developing key knowledge of a subject. A great example of this would be to develop an understanding of a specific subject you will be teaching.

Observation of others

Live observation is great but hard, particularly when you are watching someone who is an expert. Observing alongside a mentor or peer can help you to focus on the specifics. There is also value in watching videos of teaching; this allows you to pause and look at specific actions, which is much harder in a live setting.

Figure 17.1 Professional development opportunities

The overview in Figure 17.1 gives an insight into the significant array of development opportunities available to new and experienced teachers. We explore some of them in more detail throughout this chapter, namely coaching and mentoring, conferences and workshops, reflection, networks, and deliberate practice. We have chosen these not because they are necessarily the most effective or important, but because they are the most common.

HOW TO MAKE THE MOST OUT OF MENTORING OR COACHING

We take mentoring as the precise actions that a novice will undertake supported and advised by an expert. Coaching is more about the support provided to more expert colleagues to develop their practice even further. Coaching requires the coachee to have a schema and the reflective ability to identify issues and the dialogue for the coachee to implement the outputs of the discussion.

HOW TO PREPARE FOR A MENTOR MEETING

Review any notes or actions from your last meeting with them. If you haven't been able to complete everything, be honest, but also plan for when you will so you can show proactivity.

Identify three successes since your last meeting (these can be small).

Choose one area you want help with during your time with your mentor. Be as specific as possible and link it to your current areas for development. For example, if in a recent observation some of your feedback focused on needing to improve your approach to establishing routines, you might choose to focus on how you get students to enter the classroom.

Be specific about how you want your mentor to help you. If you are looking at student entry routines, you might ask your mentor to rehearse this with you using deliberate practice. Or perhaps ask them if you can watch a video of another teacher doing it and discuss how you could apply the strategies you see.

Write down your three biggest priorities for the coming week, and consider any concerns you have and want to discuss.

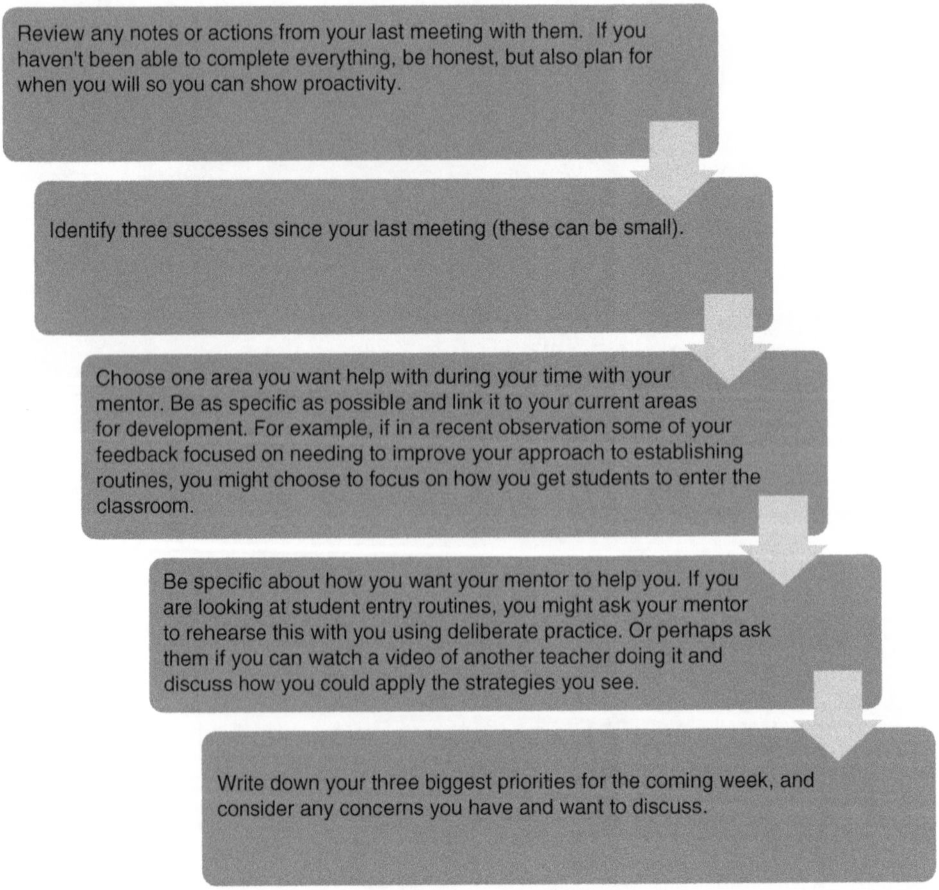

Figure 17.2   How to prepare for a mentor meeting

What is really useful about the above is that you, as the early career teacher, are taking responsibility for your own development and you are ensuring precision on particular areas on which to focus (see Figure 17.2). If we as teachers focus on trying to fix too many things at the same time, we end up doing none of them well. If you can be precise, then your mentor can also advise on which order you should tackle things.

We recommend agreeing ways of working with your mentor in your first meeting. This should be reviewed regularly too, as your needs will likely change throughout the process. The relationship between you and your mentor is one of the most important you will have, so it's worth investing the time in getting this right.

Having a shared agenda really helps in keeping focus throughout the meeting (see Table 17.1). It also ensures you are both able to prepare in advance, so you get the most out of the time together. Using tools such as Google Docs or OneNote will mean you can have a shared place to store these.

Table 17.1   *Suggested mentor meeting agenda template*

Item *Complete this in advance of the meeting.*	Notes *Use this space to write notes during the meeting.*	Actions *Use this space to make a note of specific actions - remember to put a deadline!*
How are you? (5 minutes) *Wellbeing is important for both you and your mentor, so always start the meeting with a short update on how you are and any concerns you have.*		
Actions from last meeting (5 minutes) *In this section, you should list out any actions you agreed in your last meeting with a short comment on whether they have been completed or not.*		
Successes since last meeting (5 minutes) *It's useful to start with this so you can recognise the progress you are making and celebrate this with your mentor. Think about what it was, but also what the ingredients were of the success. This means you can apply this to other areas that are less successful. Try to list three successes.*		
Development focus (30 minutes) *Write down what you want to focus on and how you want your mentor to support you. Your mentor may also have suggestions for how this is done. Some schools will have specific processes they use (e.g. instructional coaching).*		

(Continued)

Table 17.1 (Continued)

Item Complete this in advance of the meeting.	Notes Use this space to write notes during the meeting.	Actions Use this space to make a note of specific actions – remember to put a deadline!
Priorities for next week (10 minutes) Try to identify three key priorities for the next week you would like to review or discuss with your mentor.		
Wrap up (5 minutes) Agree actions and date/time of next meeting.		

HOW TO PREPARE FOR AND GET THE MOST FROM CONFERENCES OR WORKSHOPS

There are a huge number of conferences and workshops available for teachers, some of which you will probably receive at school as part of in-service training (INSET) or after-school training. In addition to these, organisations such as ResearchEd and subject associations offer a range of training, much of which is affordable. One of the hardest things about attending conferences or workshops is finding the time to go, whether this is agreeing to be released from school or attending in the evenings or at weekends.

First (and probably most importantly), make sure you are choosing to attend something that is linked to your areas for development. You will be speaking regularly with your mentor about your development, so if there is something that continues to come up, then it might be worth considering some additional training to complement the day-to-day development you undertake in school/college.

Once you have chosen the right course/conference or workshop to meet your needs, you will benefit from spending some time being explicit about what you hope to learn from it, and how this learning will impact your teaching practice. It is definitely worth discussing this with your mentor, particularly if you will need time away from school or if there are opportunities for your school to contribute to the costs.

KEY QUESTIONS

Take time at the conference to meet other delegates and discuss the input. This helps you to generate further ideas on who to see but also helps you to begin the reflection process. Consider the following:

- Is there agreement on that approach?

- Are there criticisms?

- How valid are they?

- How should I adapt these aspects to my context?

- How could I run a small test before doing it with all my classes to see what I find out?

It is important that we are all open to training and advice alongside being critical consumers of this.

HOW TO REFLECT ON YOUR PRACTICE TO HELP YOU IMPROVE

Finlay (2008) describes reflective practice as 'learning through, and from, experience towards gaining new insights of self and practice' (p1). No doubt you will spend a lot of your time thinking about your lessons and speaking about them to your colleagues (or friends/parents/partners/strangers/the local shopkeeper) in the early stages of your career. I am also sure you will have heard about the importance of becoming a 'reflective practitioner' throughout your ITT programme. Reflecting, though, takes time, and time is something that will be in short supply. So, how can you do it simply and effectively?

KEY QUESTIONS

- *What?* Write an account of what happened. Try to choose a section of a lesson (ideally something you are trying to improve) rather than the whole thing.

- *So what?* Consider what this means. It's useful to draw upon literature here, or you might want to discuss with your mentor.

- *Now what?* Arguably, the most useful part of any reflection. Consider what you will do differently in your practice as a result of this experience.

HOW YOU CAN BENEFIT FROM NETWORKS

Thanks to social media, the great networks that have been in the system for a while can be amplified. These might be subject- or phase-specific or they might be around a particular area of professional practice. Some networks are face-to-face and bolstered online, and some are online most of the time and bolstered by in-person debate on a few occasions. It may be that you build your own network either in school or across a few schools. It could be as simple as asking what the big challenges are and how others have solved them.

There is huge value in networks to share knowledge and expertise and to discuss challenges. However, terms need to be used with precision. If they are not, then practice does not change or remains unchallenged. In an effective network, precision should be built in. This is alongside the trust that needs to be built among a group to give honest context to resolve a problem.

The Chartered College of Teaching is, of course, a great way in which to connect both in person and virtually with colleagues across the country for professional dialogue. If you have an idea for discussion, then suggest it. If you are wrestling with something, then you can almost guarantee that others are too, and that someone, somewhere has some first-hand advice on how they have resolved it. The subject associations are also a great place to go. Many produce high-quality publications where both the subject itself and the pedagogy are discussed. Given the discussions around knowledge-rich curricula, this becomes ever-more important. They are also wonderful signposts to conferences and colleagues doing interesting work or research. Social media can also be a great resource for discussion and signposting to high-quality reading and materials.

HOW TO PRACTISE

Ericsson (2006) shows how practice can enhance performance, particularly for novices. Deans for Impact (2016) outlines how and why this can be best utilised as part of teacher preparation. The best practice you will experience is done with an expert. Using time with your mentor to deliberately practise is one of the most valuable things you can do. However, it is unlikely your mentor will be available for regular or long periods of time, so practising independently is something that can be of huge value. Here are some tips for doing it right:

1. Identify what you are going to practise. You need to be specific, alongside choosing something that is going to help you develop. Look through your recent feedback and choose one thing you need to improve. As an example, this could be, 'I need to improve how I use cold call to ensure all of my students are thinking of the answer'.

2. Once you have identified something specific to practise, you need to find an example of this being done well.

3. Next, decide the scenario you are going to use. It probably makes sense to practise for an upcoming lesson if you can. You will also need to script what you are going to say.

4. Get ready! Ideally, you should practise to make it as realistic as possible. If you can, doing it in a classroom is best. If you are practising something that requires you to stand up and walk around, make sure you have the space to do so. You want to make it as realistic as possible. See it as a kind of dress rehearsal (without the costumes!). You'll also want a way of knowing how you've done. The best way is to record yourself (buying a phone stand would be a pretty good investment) and make sure you can pick up the recording. If you can't record, try to do it in front of a mirror.

5. Use your script to have a go. It will feel strange at first, no doubt, but your students and you will both benefit.

6. Review how you did. It's probably worth going back to the best practice example you looked at first to refresh your memory. Then watch the video of yourself (or try to remember what you did, if you weren't able to do this). When watching, think about how clear your language was, how you used body language, and if your pace was right. Compare your rehearsal to the expert example and write down one or two things you will change next time.

7. Repeat (at least once) until you feel you are close enough to the expert example and/or you have had enough. Practice can be hard work, so don't feel disheartened if after three or four runs through you want to move on to something else.

This whole cycle should only take around 30 minutes (depending on what you are practising). It will probably be shorter once you have done it a few times.

CONCLUSION

Professional learning and growth are some of the most important tools we have as educators to make a difference to student progress. However, it is not easy and takes time. As early career teachers, your development trajectory can be incredibly steep if it can be prioritised. We recognise the complexity of this, but hopefully this chapter has provided you with a few small tools and techniques which will make it just that little bit easier for you.

KEY CONCEPTS AND FURTHER READING

GENERAL CPD

Chartered College of Teaching CPD packs on a range of topics: **https://impact.chartered.college/category/cpd-packs/**

The TES Institute has a range of online courses: **www.tes.com/institute/cpd-courses-teachers**

MAKING THE MOST OUT OF MENTORING AND COACHING

Lofthouse, R. (2018) *Mentoring*. Available at: https://impact.chartered.college/article/lofthouse-virtuous-circle-mentoring/

- This article offers advice to help you make the most of mentoring.

REFLECTING ON YOUR PRACTICE

Tripp, D. (1993) *Critical Incidents in Teaching: Developing Professional Judgement*. London: Routledge.

- This book includes strategies to help you reflect critically on your teaching and develop your professional judgement.

BENEFITING FROM NETWORKS

Vangrieken, K., Dochy, F., Raes, E. and Kyndt, E. (2015) Teacher collaboration: a systematic review. *International Research Review*, 15: 17–40.

- This paper discusses the benefits of teacher collaboration for students, teachers and schools, as well as the barriers to, and enablers of, effective collaboration.

REFERENCES

Deans for Impact (2016) *Practice with Purpose: The Emerging Science of Teacher Expertise*. Available at: https://deans-forimpact.org/wp-content/uploads/2016/12/Practice-with-Purpose_FOR-PRINT_113016.pdf

Ericsson, K.A. (2006) The influence of experience and deliberate practice on the development of superior expert performance. In K.A. Ericsson, N. Charness, P.J. Feltovich and R.R. Hoffman (eds), *The Cambridge Handbook of Expertise and Expert Performance*. Cambridge: Cambridge University Press, pp683–703.

Finlay, L. (2008) Reflecting on 'Reflective Practice'. Available at: http://ncsce.net/wp-content/uploads/2016/10/Finlay-2008-Reflecting-on-reflective-practice-PBPL-paper-52.pdf

Pink, D.H. (2009) *Drive: The Surprising Truth about What Motivates Us*. New York: Riverhead Books.

ENGAGING WITH RESEARCH

MARK ENSER

HEAD OF GEOGRAPHY AND RESEARCH LEAD, HEATHFIELD COMMUNITY COLLEGE, EAST SUSSEX, UK

INTRODUCTION

It can sometimes feel that educational research is a confusing field. If we aren't careful, we can fall into the narrative that there is simply too much contradictory advice out there and that this advice is subject to constant change. However, this ignores the vital role that we as professionals play in the process; as teachers, we take this research and put it into the context of the classroom. Sorting out this conflicting advice and making sense of it is a part of our job.

CHAPTER OBJECTIVES

This chapter will enable you to:

- understand the challenges and opportunities of educational research;
- identify, review and assess sources of educational research;
- understand how educational research might look in the classroom, and how you might implement research findings in your setting.

WHAT IS EDUCATIONAL RESEARCH FOR?

One of the most powerful defences of the use of educational research comes from Carl Hendrick, who contends that there is:

an ethical imperative to provide the best possible classroom conditions in which the students in our charge can flourish. This means rejecting what wastes time and embracing that which make the most use of it. It's difficult to think of another serious profession that has so willfully discarded evidence and embraced the transient and the facile as much as education has.

(Hendrick and McPherson, 2017, p11)

He acknowledges that this research may not provide all the answers, but it does at least give us a 'road map to avoid the dead-ends and backroads of faddism and misinformation' (p11).

This issue of the research not providing all the answers is one often highlighted by Gert Biesta, who has pointed out that a big problem with the question of 'what works' in education is that we first have to establish what we want it to work *for*. He also expresses concern that an obsession with 'what works' can lead to teachers being granted less agency in the classroom as it is assumed that there is some sort of definitive answer. Once we say, 'This works best', it behoves us all to do it (Biesta, 2007).

However, educational research should not be seen as something to replace teacher experience, but rather as something to enhance it. As Jonathan Firth (2019) argues, 'Realistically, research cannot replace experience – if it could, then it would be possible to train the perfect teacher simply by exposing them to the theory and research evidence' (p10). However, he goes on to remind us that experience alone is also not enough, as experienced teachers can still harbour misconceptions about how learning works. This theme is picked up by David Didau (2015), who demonstrates that many myths about education remain and that personal experience can often be an unreliable guide to truth.

Perhaps, then, we can see that educational research should *inform* our practice as teachers by pointing us in the direction of what is likely to work, but that we shouldn't necessarily seek to base our practice entirely on this research. There are a number of limitations of educational research that we should be aware of. For example, Pedro De Bruyckere et al. (2019) point out, 'Research is carried out within a particular context, but there is no certainty that the results will be replicated in a different context' (p152). We should keep in mind a number of methodological issues with the way educational research is carried out and reported. As such, we should be cautious of picking up on the findings of any one study and assuming we can base our decision-making in the classroom upon it. Instead, we should reflect on its potential to inform the decisions we take.

KEY QUESTIONS

Consider a piece of educational research.

- Does it challenge you to think differently about assumptions you hold?
- Might it lead to you finessing something you already do?
- Is it worth trialling? If so, how will you evaluate its impact?

WHERE CAN YOU FIND THE RESEARCH?

Educational research has never been so available to teachers. The rise of social media means that teachers are able to share papers they have read and discuss their implications; this is taken further by free blogging platforms that have helped to remove gatekeepers from publishing and enable a greater range of voices to be heard. However, this is not without risk. Pam Jarvis (2019) has argued, 'Blogs based purely on the personal experiences and opinions of one person may be presented by some writers (and consumed by some readers) on the same basis as more in-depth, academic peer reviewed publications'. Luckily, teaching is a graduate profession and teachers are able to both read and write about the subject of educational research from a critical perspective. Many teacher-writers are careful to cite the research they are reflecting on, and the medium means that peer discussion is encouraged.

An exploration of research-informed approaches to teaching is also found at educational conferences, both in more formal settings (such as those organised by ResearchEd) and more informal ones (such as the recent BrewEd movement originally organised by Daryn Egan-Simon and Ed Finch). These give an opportunity for teachers to meet and discuss their practice, sharing what they are doing and why.

Original research papers are also becoming more available. Membership of the Chartered College of Teaching gives access to academic research and the organisation publishes its own peer-reviewed journal, *Impact*. Subject associations also usually produce their own journals of both academic and practical writing aimed at teachers in the classroom. All of this helps in that process of contextualising research for our settings and exploring its wider implications.

Another move that is helping to make educational research more accessible to teachers is the rise in the appointment of a *research lead* in schools. This role involves a teacher acting as the interface between the world of educational research and that of their colleagues in school. Tom Bennett (2016) suggests, 'Put simply, the Research Lead can connect the school to the greater world of educational research, while simultaneously acting as a filter' (p10). This 'filter' is an important part of the role. As we have just seen, research might be increasingly available, but this creates its own issue. For a busy teacher, the sheer volume of research can seem an insurmountable barrier to seeking the answers or guidance it could provide. Where the role is well used, it provides someone with the time to seek out the research sought by other people in school and even to start the process of translating it into a usable form for people in the classroom.

For those schools without the capacity to create their own research leads, the Education Endowment Foundation (EEF), and the Research Schools Network that they have funded, helps to fill that gap. The EEF website contains a number of very useful guides to implementing aspects of educational research (on topics such as metacognition or whole-school literacy), and they provide a summary of the impact of a range of possible educational practices such as homework, ability-setting and feedback. The research schools are placed around the country and offer services such as continuing professional development (CPD) on research-informed topics.

HOW MIGHT THE USE OF THIS RESEARCH LOOK IN THE CLASSROOM?

The availability of educational research means very little if it doesn't lead to a benefit in the classroom. In the final part of this chapter, we will look at three examples of how being informed by research may help us to answer some questions about our practice with the aim of helping our students to learn.

CAN I USE QUESTIONING AS A FORM OF RETRIEVAL PRACTICE?

One of the most secure areas of educational research is on the benefits of the *testing effect*, whereby practising the retrieval of information makes it easier to retrieve again in the future (see Karpicke and Grimaldi, 2012). Many teachers take advantage of this testing effect by incorporating retrieval activities such as low-stakes quizzes into their lessons (Enser, 2018), but teachers may also seek to benefit from the testing effect through the asking of questions during the lesson. For example, when teaching pupils about Shakespeare's use of language in *Macbeth*, the teacher might ask a pupil, 'What quote helps to show how the writer was attempting to portray Lady Macbeth's state of mind?' The hope would be that the pupil would recall the quote, boosting its retrieval strength, and that the rest of the class would go through the process with them. But will this happen?

Research by Magdalena Abel and Henry Roediger suggests that it is not that simple. Their work shows that only the pupil answering the question is going to go through the important process of attempting to retrieve the information needed and so benefit from the testing effect. Even if the rest of the class are asked to monitor this student's answer closely and consider if they are right or not, they don't see a benefit. They haven't had to retrieve the information themselves (Abel and Roediger, 2018). So, what does the research suggest we as teachers might do in response?

One solution would be to pose the question to the whole class, wait for everyone to try to form an answer, and then ask one pupil, seemingly at random, to answer it. The intention here is that everyone has had to go through the retrieval process as they do not know who will be called upon to answer. Although this is often considered good practice, it can be very difficult to break long-established habits of calling on a pupil before asking a question or not giving pupils sufficient time to think of an answer. An awareness of the underpinning research may help us to break these habits.

HOW CAN I HELP MY PUPILS TO STUDY EFFECTIVELY?

There has been a long-held belief that everyone needs to find their own way to revise and that what works for one person may not work for another. Research by John Dunlosky, however, challenges this idea and suggests that there are certain common principles that separate more and less effective practice. He also suggests that students are not very good at identifying and choosing these more effective methods (Dunlosky, 2013).

His research suggests that common methods deployed by students, such as rereading their notes, highlighting or writing summaries, simply doesn't involve enough hard thinking for them to derive any benefits. What they do is provide a feeling of comfort; rereading notes makes them seem familiar, and therefore like students are making progress. Instead, we need to ask our students to engage in the more uncomfortable practice of self-quizzing, where they attempt to answer questions without reference to their notes. We should also ask them to distribute this practice throughout the course, and not see revision as something to do just before a test or exam.

This has many implications for us as teachers. We might decide that as pupils are likely to select less effective study methods, we should explicitly teach them why the more effective methods will work. We might also decide to take more charge of their study process and begin setting self-testing-style homework throughout the year rather than simply setting 'revise' as a homework before a test.

WHY DO SOME STUDENTS SEEM TO BECOME 'STUCK'?

Two economics lecturers, Erik Meyer and Ray Land, discovered that sometimes they'd have students who seemed to be making good progress but then would become stuck at a certain point and struggle thereafter. They used this experience to identify what they termed *threshold concepts* – troublesome knowledge that students needed to understand before progressing further in the curriculum. They suggested that these threshold concepts had certain shared characteristics, such as the ability to change the way you saw the world and a degree of permanence (i.e. once you understood them, the effect was so profound that you couldn't forget it) (Meyer and Land, 2003).

For example, in geography, we could argue that sustainability is a threshold concept. If our students don't understand this term, they will struggle to understand a lot of what comes after when looking at issues such as resource management or urban challenges. These later ideas are predicated on an understanding of this concept. Once they grasp this idea, though, it is transformative. They are able to see decisions through a prism of economic, social and environmental considerations and understand the balancing act needed to meet the needs of the present without harming the capacity of future generations to meet their own needs.

The implication for us in the classroom is to consider the role of threshold concepts in our own subjects. Can we identify them? Having identified them, can we ensure we focus our teaching on their mastery? Can we then assess whether pupils have grasped them and, if not, respond in some way before moving on?

CONCLUSION

Educational research can never provide the answer to how we should teach. What it can do is point us towards the answers to more specific questions about aspects of classroom practice. An awareness of this research shouldn't remove the agency of teachers to make their own decisions about what is best for their classes; instead, it should inform this agency and help us to ensure we reflect on our own practice to find ways to improve. This sits at the heart of what it means to be a professional.

KEY QUESTIONS

- What research from your time training to teach has stayed with you as you begin your teaching career?

- What do you wish educational research would be able to tell you?

- Where might you find the answers to these questions?

- What barriers do you think stand in the way of teaching becoming a more informed profession?

- How might you overcome these barriers?

KEY CONCEPTS AND FURTHER READING

THE 'WHAT WORKS' DEBATE

Barton, C. and Bennett, T. (2019) *The ResearchEd Guide to Educational Myths: An Evidence-Informed Guide for Teachers*. Woodbridge: John Catt Educational.

Biesta, G. (2007) Why what works won't work. *Educational Theory*, 57(1): 1–22.

Hendrick, C. and McPherson, H. (2017) *What Does This Look Like in the Classroom?* Woodbridge: John Catt Educational.

- These books inform the 'what works' debate in education, discussing the challenges of, and opportunities afforded by, applying the findings of education research in the classroom.

RESEARCH-INFORMED PRACTICE

De Bruyckere, P., Kirschner, P.A. and Hulshof, C. (2019) *More Urban Myths about Learning and Education*. London: Routledge.

Didau, D. (2015) *What if Everything You Knew about Education Was Wrong?* Carmarthen: Crown House.

Enser, M. (2019) *Teach Like Nobody's Watching*. Carmarthen: Crown House.

- These books clarify the evidence base around research-informed practice, dispelling myths and contradictory advice to help you develop efficient, effective teaching strategies.

COGNITIVE LOAD THEORY

Boxer, A. (2019) *Challenge Beyond Bloom*. Available at: https://achemicalorthodoxy.wordpress.com/2019/10/23/challenge-beyond-blooms/

Karpicke, J.D. and Grimaldi, P.J. (2012) Retrieval-based learning: a perspective for enhancing meaningful learning. *Educational Psychology Review*, 24: 401–18.

Shibli, D. and West, R. (2018) *Cognitive Load Theory and Its Application in the Classroom*. Available at: https://impact.chartered.college/article/shibli-cognitive-load-theory-classroom/

- These sources discuss the research behind cognitive load theory and the implications for classroom practice.

REFERENCES

Abel, M. and Roediger, H.L. III (2018) The testing effect in a social setting: does retrieval practice benefit a listener? *Journal of Experimental Psychology: Applied*, 24(3): 347–59.

Bennett, T. (2016) *The School Research Lead*. Available at: www.educationdevelopmenttrust.com/Education DevelopmentTrust/files/93/93c332a4-40df-41ac-8a9b-f803c6573d10.pdf

Biesta, G. (2007) Why what works won't work. *Educational Theory*, 57(1): 1–22.

De Bruyckere, P., Kirschner, P.A. and Hulshof, C. (2019) *More Urban Myths about Learning and Education.* London: Routledge.

Didau, D. (2015) *What if Everything You Knew about Education Was Wrong?* Carmarthen: Crown House.

Dunlosky, J. (2013) Strengthening the student toolbox. *American Educator*, 37(3): 12–21.

Enser, M. (2018) *Retrieval Practice: Five New Tips to Make Learning Stick.* Available at: www.tes.com/news/retrieval-practice-five-new-tips-make-learning-stick

Firth, J. (2019) *The Teacher's Guide to Research.* London: Routledge.

Hendrick, C. and McPherson, H. (2017) *What Does This Look Like in the Classroom?* Woodbridge: John Catt Educational.

Jarvis, P. (2019) *The Edu-Blogger, the School and the Academy.* Available at: www.bera.ac.uk/blog/the-edublogger-the-school-and-the-academy

Karpicke, J.D. and Grimaldi, P.J. (2012) Retrieval-based learning: a perspective for enhancing meaningful learning. *Educational Psychology Review*, 24: 401–18.

Meyer, J.H.F. and Land, R. (2003) Threshold concepts and troublesome knowledge: linkages to ways of thinking and practising within the disciplines. In C. Rust (ed.), *Improving Student Learning: Theory and Practice Ten Years On.* Oxford: Oxford Centre for Staff and Learning Development, pp 412–24.

19

MANAGING YOUR WELLBEING

BUKKY YUSUF

SENIOR LEADER AND HEAD OF SCIENCE, EDITH KAY SCHOOL, LONDON, UK

INTRODUCTION

During the last five years in the UK, discussions regarding education and teachers have frequently included the terms 'workload', 'wellbeing' and 'work-life balance'. Part of this is due to feedback shared via the Department for Education (DfE), wherein 'most teachers said they could not complete their workload within the working week and that they did not have a good work-life balance' (Teacher Toolkit, 2019).

The inclusion of 'managing workload and wellbeing' in the Early Career Framework (ECF) provides emphasis for you to include these as part of your professional development, because this is something that needs to be constantly managed during the first few years of teaching in order to undertake the role as best as you can.

Therefore, the aim of this chapter is to help you to build, maintain and sustain the foundations of your wellbeing throughout your teaching career. It will help you to prioritise those things that will make the biggest difference to the outcomes of your students. It will do this by sharing practical advice and suggestions that specifically link to section 8 of the ECF, 'Professional Behaviours'.

CHAPTER OBJECTIVES

In this chapter, you will learn:

- the importance of wellbeing and work-life balance (how you can protect your time for rest and recovery);
- strategies that help to reduce workload;
- effective time management strategies (systems and routines to support efficient time and task management);
- collaboration strategies that help to share planning/preparation loads and shared resources.

THE IMPORTANCE OF WELLBEING AND WORK-LIFE BALANCE

For many, teaching is a vocation where we tend to give and do as much as we possibly can in order to help our students to progress as well as they can. Since our time, energy and internal resources are finite, this stance can lead to eventually burning out.

In order to help avoid burnout, we need to explore what the terms 'wellbeing' and 'work-life balance' mean:

Wellbeing – the state of being comfortable, healthy, or happy.

Work-life balance – the division of one's time and focus between working and family or leisure activities.

(Lexico, 2019a, 2019b)

Even if your school supports the wellbeing and work-life balance of every person within it, you *must* be clear about what these terms mean to you, because we all interpret them in different ways.

KEY QUESTIONS

Here are a few questions to help you consider, define and deduce what this means in relation to your life as a newly qualified teacher (NQT):

- What does wellbeing and work-life balance mean to you?

- What are the things, outside of your role, that help you to unwind and switch off from school?

- What helps you to recharge?

- When do you undertake these things?

- What strategies will you put in place to ensure you safeguard the time you put aside for your wellbeing and work-life balance?

In spite of how busy teachers generally are, it almost seems paradoxical to realise that unless you have time to do things that make you feel comfortable, healthy or happy, you are less effective in your role, which in turn can have a knock-on effect on the quality of teaching and learning undertaken in your classroom.

In his Sizzle podcast interview with Lesha Small (The Sizzle Podcast, 2019), Dr Jo Taylor shared advice given to him by his mentor Dame Mary Marsh, the first director of the Clore Social Leadership Programme (an initiative to develop leaders who transform their communities through social change): 'Know yourself. Be yourself. Look after yourself.' So, while Jo worked at school, he was primed, and recognised what his limit was. He valued this piece of advice to start in the world of teaching.

As an early career teacher, the most important aspect of your role, besides putting the key aspects in place for your students to be as successful as they can, is carving out and safeguarding time for yourself. You have to accept that there will never be enough time to do all the things you are expected to do, want to do, or do as well as you want to do them. So, you need to get used to the concept of 'satisficing' (*The Economist*, 2009), a hybrid of the terms 'satisfy' and 'suffice', which means 'good enough'. Not everything needs to be done at 100 per cent. The more you take care of yourself, the more energy you will have for your role. It may sound paradoxical, but it is true.

If you search on social media for terms related to eudemonia, you will find a plethora of links to this and a dizzying array of advice, as well as examples of what educators do to maintain their wellbeing and work-life balance.

However, it's essential that you:

- define what these terms mean for you;

- explore what works best for you in maintaining your own personal wellbeing and work-life balance.

Whenever I have presented about wellbeing and work-life balance, there's one question I always ask: 'There are 168 hours in a week. How many are spent on time for yourself or your nearest and dearest?' Deducting time for sleep, travel, planning and marking leaves only a few hours. Yet many of us do not even spend this amount of time ensuring that we are as healthy as we can be. Saving this time for the half-term breaks or major holidays is simply not enough.

STRATEGIES THAT HELP TO REDUCE WORKLOAD

If you were to ask teachers which activities take up most of their time, marking would be a frequent response, accompanied with groans. It is not unusual for your whole evening or weekend to be taken up with marking, especially for subjects that teach a higher number of classes than others and when you have tight deadlines to mark assessments.

Below are some of the strategies that I have used to help reduce marking workloads, and which help to progress the learning of your students no matter their age or ability:

- autocorrect function;

- books left open at last page;

- dot marking;

- Google Forms;

- highlighting comments;

- whole-class feedback template;

- peer assessment bookmarks;

- peer/self-assessment statements;

- stickers for feedback/learning activities;

- visualisers.

We will go through a selection of strategies to help you consider the practical applications for each, and to evaluate which might work best in your school setting.

AUTOCORRECT FUNCTION

You can use Microsoft's autocorrect feature to create your own comment banks when marking work or writing reports. Using this functionality can improve the quality of your written comments and also speed up your marking, saving you precious time. Furthermore, the autocorrect lists you create can be used across all the Office programmes that support the autocorrect feature.

You will first need to review what you plan to mark or reports you intend to write, to note the key words, terms or phrases that you will be using. Note down easy-to-remember codes that will be used to represent your key words, terms or phrases. For example, the code 'A1' could be used to represent the phrase, 'Your next steps are to show the working out for each calculation you completed'.

Have a Word document open and follow the sequence:

File – Options – Proofing – Autocorrect Options

Halfway down the call-out box, you will see 'Replace' and 'With'.

In the 'Replace' box, add in your code (i.e. 'A1'), and in the 'With' box add in your phrases.

Every time you type the code 'A1', the phrase will then appear. Note that the codes are case-sensitive, so entering 'a1' will not retrieve your chosen key words or phrases.

BOOKS LEFT OPEN AT LAST PAGE

This easy strategy will shave off time in having to go through a class set of books to locate the last piece of work your students worked on.

DOT MARKING

This time-saving activity utilises 8 mm sticky coloured dots to provide feedback to every student as they undertake written learning activities during your lesson. In order to maximise its effectiveness, you need to share the criteria for each coloured dot with your class. For example, a red dot represents incomplete work or inaccurate answers, a yellow dot represents good written work with some details missing, and a green dot represents excellent work with a lot of relevant detail. I introduced this to my teaching groups via PowerPoint, having a poster display in the classroom as a reminder, and even having a smaller version of the poster stuck on the inside cover of the students' exercise books.

The dots make it easy to ensure that every student is seen and has feedback to act upon in the lesson. Where written updates are required from the student, this can be completed in the colours that your school stipulates for their student feedback/self-assessment.

You can search the hashtag #dotmarking on Twitter to see more examples of this technique in action.

GOOGLE FORMS

Not only can the use of Google Forms (or equivalent alternatives such as Microsoft Forms) help to save you time; it can also be used to foster independent learning. If it is not possible to use Google Forms within your lesson, then it can easily be used to set homework.

Google Forms allows you to make assignments/surveys with different types of responses for questions, such as short answers, long answers, multiple-choice, or drop-down menus, for a variety of ways to review student learning (e.g. class surveys, short quizzes, retrieval practices). Responses provided by your students can be tracked and collated on a spreadsheet to chart progress. Even though it may take some time to set up, the time you save in the long run makes it a worthwhile tool to reduce your workload. For instance, you can set pop quizzes, multiple-choice exam questions or spelling tests with auto-graded responses.

VISUALISERS

These tools can be used to demonstrate model answers during the lesson, particularly when using the 'I do, we do, you do' strategy. This minimises preparation time for you.

EFFECTIVE TIME MANAGEMENT STRATEGIES

KEY QUESTIONS

- During the school day, when are you most effective?
- Which are the tasks that require less than a few minutes of your time?
- Which tasks require time and focus from you? When are the best times during the working week to accomplish them?

Your answers to the questions above will help you to identify when is the most effective time for you to do your planning and marking. Anything that can be done within a few minutes should be done then and there so you can avoid adding it to your to-do list. For tasks that require more time, the pomodoro technique can really help you to focus for short periods of time (25 minutes) before taking a break. Since you are working with a timer, it will help to eliminate distractions.

In order to manage your timetable most effectively, you need to think of your time as fixed and flexible (BBC Teacher Support, 2019). Your lessons, directed meetings, form times, and so on will count towards your fixed times as you have no control over this time. Flexible time relates to any time during the school day that can be used in any way you want. Your flexible times link to your planning, preparation and assessment (PPA) and non-contact time, and any tasks you aim to complete must be planned beforehand. For example, periods when your class undertakes internal in-class assessments in silence could be used to complete marking.

The RAG123 marking system (Lister, 2019) could be used to prioritise marking you can quickly tackle if it is also combined with a red/amber/green tray system. Red trays denote feedback from students where they share what they have not understood within a lesson. Amber trays highlight student feedback, outlining what they understood and what they still don't understand. A question could be posed to help students unpick the aspects that they did not understand. Green tray feedback can be used to set preset extension questions that can be glued or stuck into the students' exercise books.

Discipline and a certain level of persistence are required to maximise your time.

You also need to consider which days of your working week provide the most opportunities to move forward with your priorities and which days are unrealistic (i.e. when you are teaching all day). In addition, explore when during the school day you can complete what needs to be done without interruptions.

In order to help you prioritise what needs to be done, you can use the must/should/could approach to help you cut through the list of things that could be actioned.

KEY QUESTIONS

- What are three things that must be done by the end of today? (These are your key priorities.)
- Which three things should you do today? (These can be done once your priorities are completed.)
- Which three things could you do? (These are not priorities, so you can easily leave them for now.)

Three items for each section denotes the *maximum* number of items. Otherwise, a long list of things to do can feel stressful in itself.

Beyond all this, you have to accept that when we are tired or unwell, we tend to be less efficient with our time management. Being sleep-deprived will also have a significant impact on your time management.

TRANSLATE IN GOOGLE SHEETS

To save time translating key words, glossaries and learning resources into different languages for students that require them, you can use the Google Translate formula within Google Sheets. Jake Miller demonstrates how easily this can be done: **https://jakemiller.net/translate-in-google-sheets/**

COLLABORATION STRATEGIES THAT HELP TO SHARE PLANNING/PREPARATION

KEY QUESTIONS

- How do you use your non-contact time?

- When do you do your planning? Who do you do your planning with? How can you cut down your time on effective planning?

Just as you schedule time for meetings, get into the habit of scheduling protected time for yourself or collaborations with colleagues during the school week. Planning as part of a team or pair can help to increase your levels of productivity and wellbeing. Some schools/departments/phases formally organise collaborative planning as part of meeting times and during PPA/non-contact periods. Collaborative planning can be shared so that teachers create lesson plans/schemes based upon their strengths or specific topics, which are shared across the team. This way, everyone gets a full curriculum of teaching resources with less time spent planning it. Co-planning allows you to learn tips, tricks and strategies that work from your colleagues. Some of these in themselves can reduce the time spent on planning.

If your school does not do this on a formal basis, it can be something that is implemented with a planning buddy to share the workload. Furthermore, you can spend more time increasing your knowledge base and understanding of the topic(s) you will teach and building your confidence with the learning activities you set the students. In order to be most confident, we should complete the work that we set our students in advance – this will help in your explanations and with the questions you plan to orally ask. Beyond this, to avoid reinventing the wheel if there is nothing in place that you can use to plan lessons, you can collaborate virtually with UK-based educators online.

There are a diverse range of educational groups on Twitter that constantly share lesson resources and planning ideas. These include:

- @PrimaryRocks

- @UKEdChat

- @ASTsupportAli

- @TeamEnglish1

- @TeamScience

- @LessonToolbox

- @JiveSpin

- @87History

- @mathsjem

- @Mr_Minchin

There are also groups on Facebook, such as Primary Teachers, a private (group members only) forum where ideas and resources are shared.

Even though there are a number of social media platforms that can be used to share and receive resources, make the time to find the platform that works best for you.

CONCLUSION

The more you engage in conversations with various educators about ways in which we can manage our workload and wellbeing, the more you will realise that beyond common general approaches, the diverse range of strategies highlights that we all have different approaches based on our individual understanding of these terms. During your early years as a teacher, it is vital that you do the same.

KEY CONCEPTS AND FURTHER READING

THE IMPORTANCE OF WELLBEING AND WORK-LIFE BALANCE

Eyre, C. (2016) *The Elephant in the Staffroom: How to Reduce Stress and Improve Teacher Wellbeing*. London: Routledge.

- Eyre's book looks at both the psychological and practical aspects of managing stress and includes prompts for reflection as well as practical advice.

STRATEGIES THAT HELP TO REDUCE WORKLOAD

Lister, K. (2019) *Teach Like You Imagined It*. Carmarthen: Crown House.

- This book contains tools and ideas to help you maximise your day-to-day productivity.

HASHTAGS TO REVIEW ON TWITTER

- #dotmarking

- #ReduceWork

- #UKEdchat

- #wholeclassmarking

─────────── **REFERENCES** ───────────

BBC Teacher Support (2019) *5 Strategies to Help You to Reclaim Your Time.* Available at: www.bbc.co.uk/teach/teacher-support/5-strategies-to-help-you-reclaim-your-time/zr98cqt

The Economist (2009) *Herbert Simon.* Available at: www.economist.com/news/2009/03/20/herbert-simon

Lexico (2019a) *Well-Being.* Available at: www.lexico.com/en/definition/well-being

Lexico (2019b) *Work-Life Balance.* Available at: www.lexico.com/definition/work-life_balance

Lister, K. (2019) *Teach Like You Imagined It.* Carmarthen: Crown House.

The Sizzle Podcast (2019) *#012: The Unexpected Leader.* Available at: https://open.spotify.com/episode/4bSPdW2m70iIEzxc6gaG3Y?si=0LWEf7IXRQ2ZsatVsq2uHw

Teacher Toolkit (2019) *Is Teacher Workload in England Improving?* Available at: www.teachertoolkit.co.uk/2019/10/19/teacher-workload-2019/

20

BUILDING EFFECTIVE RELATIONSHIPS WITH TEACHING ASSISTANTS, THE SENCO, SEND SPECIALISTS AND PARENTS/CARERS

ROB WEBSTER

CENTRE FOR INCLUSIVE EDUCATION, UCL INSTITUTE OF EDUCATION, LONDON, UK

INTRODUCTION

The Early Career Framework (ECF) is designed around how to support all students to succeed, including those with special educational needs and disabilities (SEND). You have an essential role as a teacher in meeting the needs of these students. Ensuring they can engage and achieve requires the collective effort of a range of practitioners and professionals, and of course parents/carers. Crucial to making it all happen, therefore, is knowing the various identities and roles of the wide coalition of people who support students with SEND, and how to build and maintain effective relationships with them.

CHAPTER OBJECTIVES

This chapter describes the behaviours and practices teachers must develop in order to fulfil their wider professional responsibilities. It aims to provide practical guidance to help you develop the skills required to meet the relevant practice statements specified in section 8 of the ECF. With reference to the best available evidence, you will:

- learn about the contribution of teaching assistants (TAs) in supplementing your teaching, and how to build effective classroom partnerships with TAs by ensuring they are effectively deployed in, and prepared for, lessons;

(Continued)

(Continued)

- learn about how to build effective working relationships with the special educational needs coordinator (SENCO) and SEND specialists, and how to access and appropriately integrate their valuable expertise into your planning and classroom practice;

- learn that building effective relationships with parents/carers and families can help maximise students' engagement and achievement, how to build and maintain effective partnerships with timely, positive communication, and the specific considerations for working with parents/carers of children with SEND.

BUILDING EFFECTIVE CLASSROOM PARTNERSHIPS WITH TAS

The long-term, international trend towards inclusion has been accompanied and assisted by an increase in the number of TAs in schools. The majority of TAs spend most of their time supporting lower-attaining students and those with SEND. This model of 'additional support for additional needs' is based on a not-unreasonable assumption: individualised support leads to positive outcomes. Yet research on the impact of TAs challenges this view.

The largest UK study of the impact of classroom support staff – the Deployment and Impact of Support Staff (DISS) project – found that students who got the most TA support performed less well academically than those who received little or no support – regardless of whether they had underlying SEND or low prior attainment (Blatchford et al., 2011).

The DISS project revealed a side effect of the support arrangement we see every day in many mainstream classes, and it is something of which teachers need to be especially mindful. Support from TAs is not really 'additional'; instead, it *replaces* time with the teacher. What happens is that the students who require high-quality teaching the most tend to receive it the least (Webster, 2017).

These effects are not attributable to TAs themselves. It is the situational and structural factors within which they work, but over which they have little or no influence, that explains the lack of impact.

There are three main things to know:

1. The first concerns TA deployment. The main explanation for the DISS project results on attainment was the way TA-supported students spent less time interacting with the teacher and became separated from the teacher and curriculum.

2. The second element is the quality of TA-to-student interaction. Compared with teacher–student interactions, TA–student interactions are less academically demanding and more task-driven. TAs tend to 'over-support' and foster dependency. They focus on getting the task completed – and completed correctly.

3. The third factor is preparedness, which relates to the training TAs have had (or not) to support learning effectively, and the training teachers have received (or not) to know how to make the most of TAs in their classrooms. Preparedness also concerns the nature and quality of planning, preparation and feedback between teachers and TAs.

A key conclusion from the DISS project is not that TAs are ineffective, but that school leaders and teachers do not always make the best decisions about how to deploy and work with them. Unlocking the potential of TAs requires effective partnerships, the best of which are characterised by seamless, fluid movements around the classroom and a clear and shared understanding of who needs to do what, with which students, and when.

PRACTICAL STRATEGIES TO BUILD AN EFFECTIVE PARTNERSHIP WITH TAS

CLASSROOM DEPLOYMENT

An essential guiding principle for teachers is that you should avoid deploying a TA as an informal teaching resource for learners with SEND. The first line of defence in raising attainment is quality, teacher-led teaching. Ensure you spend sufficient time with these students, getting to know them and their needs. There really is no better substitute for improving your teaching craft and their learning.

Think about how you can organise the classroom to ensure TAs add value to your teaching. Make sure they supplement, not replace, you. Aim to deploy TAs in ways that free up opportunities for you to work with struggling students. For example, set up the classroom in such a way that on day 1, you work with one group, the TA with another, and the other groups complete tasks collaboratively or independently. On day 2, rotate yourself, the TA and the activities, and so on throughout the week. Or you could deploy the TA in a 'triage' role. Ensure they know how to identify the students who are the most stuck and need your input to progress, and direct your attention to where your expertise is urgently needed. Some teachers give TAs a more visible role in teaching, scribing answers on the whiteboard or demonstrating equipment. This is useful for you as it allows you to maintain eye contact with the class during teaching.

The best classroom partnerships are built on a clear and specified understanding of who does what. Mapping out your roles at various stages of a lesson can help you develop and embed practices (EEF, n.d.).

SCAFFOLDING FOR INDEPENDENCE

To reiterate: students who experience high amounts of TA support are at risk of developing learned helplessness. TAs need to know how to foster student independence and ensure classroom talk focuses on the processes of learning, not products (i.e. task completion). One of the most promising ways to achieve this is based on the work of Paula Bosanquet and Julie Radford (Bosanquet et al., 2016).

Their scaffolding framework for improving TAs' interactions (see Figure 20.1; see also **maximisingtas.co.uk/ assets/content/scaffoldingframework.pdf**) recognises that it is challenging to teach independence. Instead, opportunities for students to experience and learn from it need to be created. The transformative potential of training and deploying TAs to scaffold for independence lies in another apparent contradiction: always give the least amount of help.

The TA's default position (layer 1 of the framework) is to observe student performance, allowing time and space for them to process, think and try the task independently using 'self-scaffolding' strategies. This is only possible when pupils have been taught what to do when they are stuck and have appropriate resources available to assist them.

Layer 2 of the framework is prompting. Here, TAs might intervene with a nudge or some encouragement: 'What do you need to do first?' 'What's your plan?' 'You can do this!' Layer 3 is clueing. Often students know the problem-solving strategies that prompts are designed to elicit, but they find it difficult to call them to mind. Clues are a question or small piece of information to help students to work out how to move forward. TAs should drip-feed clues, always starting with a small clue.

Layer 4 of the framework is modelling. TAs model small steps in the process to help the student move forward. There are two golden rules of modelling. First, you need to have demonstrated the steps as part of your whole-class teaching (so, technically, what TAs are doing is 'remodelling'). And second, the student needs to actively watch and listen to the TA, then try the same step for themselves afterwards.

Layer 5, correcting, is where TAs provide answers, and requires no independent thinking, and should be avoided in all but essential circumstances (e.g. where the step the student is attempting is not connected to an essential learning point).

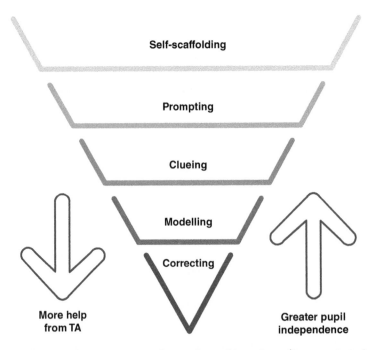

Figure 20.1   A scaffolding framework to support TAs' interactions with students (Bosanquet et al., 2016)

Pupils can practise and internalise independent learning skills over time and add them to their store of self-scaffolding techniques. But as you get to know your new class(es), you will need to ascertain whether your students have a set of strategies to help them plan, problem-solve and review their work independently, and where and how TAs can help them improve these.

LIAISON, PLANNING AND FEEDBACK

Effective teacher–TA liaison is essential to building effective classroom partnerships. It is your responsibility to ensure that TAs are prepared and are aware of the lesson 'need-to-knows' (i.e. a clear understanding of the task and the needs of specific students in relation to it). Make efficient use of any time you have with TAs by structuring conversations using an agreed checklist of things to cover.

Effective and efficient lesson planning starts with a good understanding of what students could and could not do at the end of the previous lesson. Be clear about what you want TAs to feed back. Ask them to record their observations on student performance 'live' using the scaffolding framework, such as indicating in exercise books where a student successfully self-scaffolded (SS) or was able to proceed independently following a prompt (P) or a clue (C).

Finally, TAs often deliver curriculum interventions and 'catch-up' programmes, usually outside the classroom. It is essential that you are aware of the coverage of these interventions and obtain timely feedback from TAs on students' progress and problems. Ensure that learning from outside the class is integrated into your classroom practice, and that any resources students use in the interventions are available. The key is to make explicit references to any TA-led learning outside the class so that students can make sense of and apply it in lessons.

> ## KEY QUESTIONS
>
> Building an effective classroom partnership with your TA can make a significant difference to you and your learners. Here are some points to reflect on or discuss with colleagues:
>
> - Identify three ways of organising a lesson so that the TA adds value by supplementing your teaching, not replacing you.
>
> - Develop some general prompting statements and task-specific clueing statements that TAs can use to help students manage their own learning.
>
> - What signs could you look for to check whether TAs are 'over-supporting'?

WORKING CLOSELY WITH YOUR SENCO AND OTHER SEND SPECIALISTS

In this section, we consider the wider network of SEND professionals who can offer support and advice. First, we look at the role of your school's SEND lead – the special educational needs coordinator (SENCO or SENDCO) – then we summarise the roles of a range of external specialists.

SUPPORT FROM THE SENCO

Every school, by law, must have a qualified SENCO. The SENCO has a strategic role, working with the leadership team and governing body to set the approach to teaching students with SEND and coordinating provision on the ground.

Your SENCO will know about the individual needs of students on the school's SEND register (classed as SEND support) and any students with high-level needs who have an education, health and care plan (EHCP). The SENCO leads on needs assessments and the processes of reviewing provision. They have good knowledge of the SEND code of practice and SEND-related legislation.

As a new teacher, the essential part of the SEND code of practice of which you need to be aware is this: every teacher is a teacher of students with SEND. Although the SENCO can be a 'go-to' source of professional expertise, they do not take overall responsibility for students with SEND; it is teachers who have overall responsibility for all students in their class(es).

KEY IDEAS

If you teach a student with complex SEND, seek advice from your SENCO. They can provide specialist expertise and pedagogical advice to complement your knowledge of your students. They can support you to develop your practice and ensure you meet your responsibilities towards students with SEND. Here are some ways in which your SENCO can support you:

- Invite the SENCO into your class to observe a lesson. Ask them for feedback on how students with SEND are engaging with your teaching and the curriculum coverage, and identify any potential barriers to learning.

- Swap places - you observe while the SENCO models some practical strategies to ensure students with SEND can access teaching and are fully included in lessons.

- Provide guidance and advice on types of SEND and supporting students with specific needs or conditions.

- Ask your SENCO for support with appropriate target-setting or to identify and implement effective intervention programmes.

- Your SENCO can also support you to develop your practice regarding TA deployment and preparation (see above), and liaison with parents and SEND specialists (see below).

- Your SENCO can also help with referrals or further signposting when classroom strategies do not seem to be working.

WORKING WITH OTHER SEND SPECIALISTS

As well as the SENCO, there is a large group of specialists who can support and advise you. Working with external advisors is common for students with an EHCP. Education, health and social care services are expected to collaborate on creating, implementing and reviewing the package of provision detailed in an EHCP. Families, as we will see shortly, also have a role in this process.

If you teach a student who has an EHCP or is being assessed for one, you can expect to encounter a range of external professionals and practitioners, including the following:

- *Educational psychologists (EPs).* EPs conduct specialised assessments that feed into the EHCP process. They recommend strategies to support individuals' learning and development. In many local authority areas, EPs provide staff training.

- *Speech and language therapists (SALTs).* SALTs work with students who have speech, language and communication needs (SLCN). Often they provide daily exercises or programmes for TAs to deliver. It is important that you are aware of these programmes and any targets.

- *Specialist teachers.* Often employed by local authorities, specialist teachers offer advice on classroom strategies and teaching resources for students with specific needs, such as those with a sensory impairment.

- *Health professionals.* Like specialist teachers, health professionals provide advice to schools on managing a range of different conditions.

- *Occupational therapists and physiotherapists.* Both provide rehabilitative services for students with physical needs. As with SALTs, they may train TAs to deliver daily therapeutic programmes. Again, it is important that you are aware of treatments and targets, and what you can do to support.

- *Mental health and wellbeing professionals.* There are an array of practitioners who work with students who experience challenges with social, emotional and mental health (SEMH). Some might be based in your school. Ensure you are familiar with your school's procedure for raising concerns regarding SEMH and identifying the early signs that support may be needed.

Your SENCO will provide day-to-day guidance, but visits from SEND specialists are a good opportunity to discuss recent assessments and get detailed, specific advice. If a student in your class receives visits during school hours from an external specialist, make sure you understand their role, why they are coming in, what they will be doing, and where in the building they will be working. Ensure you have access to any relevant information. Be aware of timetabling too. Ensure students are not routinely withdrawn from the same subjects, especially lessons they enjoy, as this may affect their motivation.

KEY IDEAS

SEND is a wide and complex area of education, with many specialists and specialisms. No one is expecting you to become a SEND expert within your first couple of years of teaching, but there are some small and practical steps you can take to familiarise yourself with the field.

Try this: if you teach a student with an EHCP, ask your SENCO to walk you through the sections of the student's EHCP, and the process by which it came about. A case study approach can provide a practical introduction to key terms and the roles of specialists, and it can help you prepare for the annual review to which you will contribute.

WHAT EVERY TEACHER NEEDS TO KNOW ABOUT SEND

There are two things every new teacher should know about teaching students with SEND. First, it is, in essence, no different to working out how to teach students without SEND. Spend time with individuals, discover their needs, teach to those needs, and keep your expectations high. There is a link to a practical guide to applying the graduated approach in the suggestions for further reading.

Second, you are not alone. SEND is a team effort. Collaboration leads to improved experiences and outcomes for students and provides opportunities for professional learning. Problem-solving and planning with others, observing colleagues, sharing strategies, and trying out new ideas in the classroom are both professionally rewarding and will help you hone your classroom craft.

BUILDING RELATIONSHIPS WITH PARENTS/CARERS

Parental engagement is consistently associated with academic outcomes, with positive outcomes tending to follow higher levels of engagement (Desforges and Abouchaar, 2003). There is evidence to show that improving engagement can be effective where parents' motivation is sufficiently high (Huat See and Gorard, 2015). Parents and carers of children with SEND tend to be among the most highly motivated, with reforms in 2014 leading to the family's voice having greater priority in decision-making on needs assessments and provision in the EHCP process. Yet these parents often report low levels of engagement and communication with teachers, of being distanced from decision-making about their child, and that their child is not receiving the appropriate support to help them progress (Lamb, 2009; Lindle et al., 2019).

As a teacher of students with SEND, building trusting, effective partnerships with parents, including on how to support learning at home, is essential for providing a basis for ongoing conversations about learning and development. In this final section, we consider some good practice principles for building relationships with parents. In line with the earlier point about teaching students with SEND, building relationships with parents of a child who has SEND is much like building relationships with parents of a child who does not have SEND. The guidance below will help you to develop productive partnerships with all parents.

POSITIVE PARTNERSHIPS

There is a clear value to working with parents, but it can bring challenges. Parents may hold different views about what happens in the classroom, which may reflect their own experiences of school. You may occasionally experience some pushback on your methods or decisions, but always remember the one thing you have in common with parents is that you both want to provide the child with the very best educational experience.

Parents' observations and views about their child can be rich and insightful. Finding out what a child is like at home, things they like to do and excel at, and the things they find challenging opens up new understandings and prompts ideas for new approaches in the classroom.

Take opportunities to develop a positive relationship with parents in order to build professional trust. Empathic, or active, listening goes a long way to forging that trust. From a parent's perspective, the act of the teacher giving their time and willingness to listen to you, reflecting back what they have heard, is valuable. Furthermore, in parents, you have committed partners with whom you can work together to improve things for the child.

Here is some practical advice for communicating with parents and building positive partnerships:

CHARTERED COLLEGE OF TEACHING

JOIN YOUR PROFESSIONAL BODY

We are the Chartered College of Teaching – the professional body for teachers. We are here to support you throughout your career.

CELEBRATE

Membership celebrates your commitment to the profession and dedication to being the best teacher possible. As an NQT member, you will be awarded the letters MCCT after your name to recognise your professional status.

SUPPORT

We have developed a range of research-informed publications, resources and programmes to support your professional development. NQT membership provides:

- a subscription to the print and online versions of our peer-reviewed, award-winning journal, *Impact*

- online professional development courses and CPD packs

- practical resources, including videos, research reviews and downloadable guides on MyCollege, your member-only area

- access to the world's largest education and research database.

CONNECT

We provide a space for ongoing debate and a platform for the voices of all teachers to be heard. As a member, you will receive invitations to networks, webinars and exclusive events.

STUDENT MEMBERSHIP

If you're studying to become a teacher, or you're taking time out of the classroom for full-time study, you can join for **free** as a student member. You'll get invitations to networks, webinars and events, access to resources on MyCollege and online courses, and online access to *Impact* and *The Profession*, our early career guide.

FIND OUT MORE AT: CHARTERED.COLLEGE